Our Own Image

Our Own Image

A Story of a Māori Filmmaker

Barry Barclay

Foreword by Jeff Bear

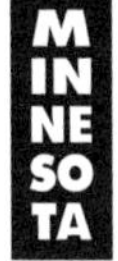

University of Minnesota Press
Minneapolis • London

*The author thanks John O'Shea, Keri Kaa, Merata Mita,
and Anne Budd for moral support and assistance
with content and detail in this book.*

Every effort was made to obtain permission to reproduce material in this book. If any proper acknowledgment has not been included, we encourage copyright holders to notify the publisher.

Originally published in 1990 by Longman Paul Limited, Auckland, New Zealand, for Shoal Bay Press

First University of Minnesota Press edition, 2015

Copyright 1990 the Estate of Barry Barclay
Copyright 2015 the Estate of Barry Barclay
Foreword copyright 2015 by the Regents of the University of Minnesota

Published by the University of Minnesota Press
111 Third Avenue South, Suite 290
Minneapolis, MN 55401–2520
http://www.upress.umn.edu

LIBRARY OF CONGRESS CATALOGING-IN-PUBLICATION DATA

Barclay, Barry. Our own image: a story of a Māori filmmaker /
Barry Barclay; foreword by Jeff Bear.
ISBN 978-0-8166-9761-8 (pb)
1. Barclay, Barry. 2. Motion picture producers and directors—
New Zealand—Biography. I. Title. PN1998.3.BA3 2015
791.4302'33092—dc23 [B]   2015006583

Printed in the United States of America on acid-free paper

The University of Minnesota is an equal-opportunity educator and employer.

22 21 20 19 18 17 16 15   10 9 8 7 6 5 4 3 2 1

Contents

Foreword: A Pistol on the Table
Jeff Bear

Barry Barclay was one of the most influential thinkers of the Fourth World. He was unique on many levels, and although I knew him only for a short time he made me feel like a long-lost brother, a comrade, a willing participant in his fascinating world of cinematic politics. He was a maverick, a curmudgeon, and a brilliant film theorist who apologized to no one.

I first met Barry Barclay in 2001 in Perth, Australia. We were both invited to show our documentaries and speak at the Australian Independent Documentary Conference (AIDC). The venue in Perth was twenty-four hours of flying time from my home in Vancouver, so I read all of the conference material and magazines that the festival had sent me, but one article that captured the views of a "radical thinker" caught my attention.

The article was about how Barclay had voiced dissent and disgust with the now-famous open pitching process in which filmmakers bring ideas to film festivals and conferences to compete in an open forum in hopes of getting their documentary ideas financed. Some film projects get lucky, and so many others are discarded. Barclay was incensed at the cultural bias, the rude behavior, and the humiliation filmmakers suffered at the cruel and often derisive comments of commissioning editors. I didn't like the process either. The activity of selling ideas about topics people don't care to hear about seemed a colossal waste of time. We were caught up in a Fourth World with Fourth World values.

The AIDC was held at a posh hotel. When I saw the price for the buffet breakfast I nearly turned away, as I was on a tight budget. But I was hungry and decided on a feast to start the day. I saw a man sitting alone and he looked Native, so I asked if I could sit with him. He said to sit while he fetched his second plate for breakfast.

After returning with a heaping plate, he held out his left hand. "Pardon the rudeness, mate, the name is Barry Barclay. Eat as much as you can. Next meal is at the reception tonight." He thought that my meals at the hotel were paid for.

Later that day we met at a designated place for a beer. He nursed his beer while I had three glasses of wine. I was at the end of my drink budget, twenty dollars per day, when another acquaintance, an American producer, showed up and offered to buy a couple of documentary filmmakers a drink. Barry quickly finished his drink and enthusiastically accepted the offered drink, but said it would be his last one as he had an early morning responsibility. We chatted about cinema, about the Maysles brothers, about indigenous rights, and drank with our American friend late into the night. Barry was a great conversationalist.

The next morning I found Barry waiting for me at the entrance to the now completely affordable buffet. We sat for hours eating and discussing a concept that by then he had coined as "Fourth Cinema." I talked about the right to tell our own stories in our own way—that it was a human right and not a privilege. I told him that our crews should be managed in a way that is respectful of our people's expectations and that the way we shoot our stories should always be tailored to the subject. After listening intently he finally slapped his hands together and said, "That's it, then. Let's go change the god damn world," and away we went.

The skeptics (and there are many) deny the reality and emergence of Fourth Cinema. Why should it not be the first cinema, our friends would lament. Why should we be number four? Mainstream colleagues merely turned their heads in dismay. At the AIDC, the indigenous people applauded Barry, but nobody hung out with him. We had been scheduled for two panel discussions, and the second round had standing room only. Barry was beside himself. I could tell by now that he had a strange habit of stroking the hair beneath his bottom lip, as if in deep contemplation of what to say next, on whom to pounce with his sharp wit and brilliant cinematic memory. He could care less about expectations of the film industry.

What the hell is this Fourth Cinema, a pakeha (white dude) asked

my friend during wine that night. At last the victim was found, and the tiger, one arm leaning forward bent as if on a hunt, pounced. Barry mounted many of these vigorous defenses that week. I thought he could easily have grown tired of making the case, but he did not. Instead I could see the fire and passion in his eyes. After a while he didn't even notice that I was studying his behavior; he merely thought of me as his Indian guide. He built one bridge at a time.

"Where shall we eat tonight?" Our American friend was on the last leg of his career and no longer worried about budgets (and had a very generous expense account, it seemed), and he asked me to pick the restaurants. He knew documentary makers were not highly paid but well researched and driven by a social conscience instead of corporate overhead. Barry was the epitome of this characteristic. He was a pauper: his T-shirts were old and had seen the washer many times over. During presentations he would be impeccably dressed, new shirt, always. His bags were also indicative of his disdain for the flash. The bags looked homemade, almost raggedy. At dinners he ate sparingly, except at breakfast and at banquets.

We traveled to the airport together at conference end. He asked me what's up next, and I said I wasn't sure. But my mind had been racing all week, caught between ideas and pragmatic things like where to turn for an income. Should I get a job? Should I return to public or private television? I blurted out that I would produce a documentary television series. He smiled and asked what the topic would be. "Haida Art—it will be partly stream of conscience [a term I heard all week long] and driven by a first person narrative." I made it all up, and as I continued to talk found myself inspired and invigorated, unaware that Barry was snoring lightly. He should have been exhausted. That was a turning point in my life although I didn't recognize it at the time. I marveled at having experienced providence in a human.

Four years would pass before I would see Barry again. He had made such an impact on my way of looking at documentary, at our own image inside the broader spectrum of the storytelling community. I attended another AIDC two years later, this time with my directing partner Marianne Jones; we attended to show our documentary

series *Ravens and Eagles: Haida Art.* Barry was not in attendance, busy engaged in the early stages of making *The Kaipara Affair,* which would turn out to be his last film. In Byron Bay we would meet Lester Bostock, who knew Barry and was a stalwart of indigenous storytelling, a pioneer among Australian aboriginal people. Lester inspired us to produce *Storytellers in Motion.*

In 2005 we traveled to New Zealand. After four years of e-mails, telephone conversations, tape exchanges, and many, many letters, Marianne and I finally accepted Barry's invitation to visit the Land of the Long White Cloud. We arrived in March as Barry was putting the final touches on the director's cut of *The Kaipara Affair,* sitting at a running time of 133 minutes. It would be a pivotal moment in the auteur's life, and we were lucky to be observers. *The Kaipara Affair* would become Barry's seminal moment, his last hoorah, the pistol on the table.

Barry was always ahead of everybody else in the indigenous movie world. He was the first indigenous person to direct a feature film. He was the first to direct a TV documentary series intended for mainstream audiences. He invented new ways of shooting interviews with long lenses so as not to seem so invasive. Māori Elders apparently appreciated this approach. He prepped for documentaries with community engagement. He tried to interview everyone who wanted to talk. He followed no script but was steadfast in covering all the bases and knowing his subject well, and he paid scant attention to television formats and time constraints.

Documentary financing was never Barry's concern. He always worked with a producer and had absolutely no interest in the business side of our vocation. In the case of *The Kaipara Affair,* his producer was none other than the legendary Don Selwyn, an old friend of Barry who was popular with the television networks. Selwyn had successfully sold the content to NZ ONAIR, and the television station wanted a ninety-minute version.

Our virgin voyage to Aotearoa came in the autumn of New Zealand's year. Everything was robust, in full harvest, and Barry had freshly received an Arts Foundation Laureate award. With some of the prize money he bought a portable DVD player to show his latest

film to people who were in it. He was showing the 133-minute version of *The Kaipara Affair* to the key players. We were his special guests at every screening, and the reception was warm without exception. Our next stop was to be at Outback Studios in Auckland.

On a hot afternoon we drove into a residential area and finally to the rear of a house, where a garage had been converted into a home-made studio. Here I met Don Selwyn, unknown to us at the time, and Davorin Fahn and Dick Reade, who were putting the finishing touches to Barry's TV film. The edit was to be viewed by Barry with his editors. After the screening he came out of the room looking as though he had seen a ghost. I had never seen this side of Barry, looking lost, uncertain, and perhaps a bit angry. I had my video camera ready to roll on his interaction with his team, but clearly something was amiss when he wouldn't let us into the screening. He waved me away, indicated for me to put my camera down. We left him alone.

Barry kept quiet that night at dinner. He was quiet throughout our drive the entire next day. He was our guide, entertained by chauffeuring us on a mini wine tour, and he guided us all the way to the home of our friend Tracey Tawhaio, where after a brief snack he was off to his next adventure. We said we would meet once more before our return to North America, but he never again pursued contact with us. Mutual friends confided that Barry would retreat from everyone from time to time.

A few months later I received my first e-mail from Barry since we said farewell at Tracey's. The message was titled "Pistol on the Table." This was his defiant moment at the travesty of the television ethos for a ninety-minute dissection of society. Barry blasted television first for adhering to commercial restraints over the public's right to know, then for taking away his creative expression. The film project could not be released in its longer version unless the television version was completed simultaneously. Barry tried to disown the film. He sought legal advice but in the end acquiesced for no other reason than simple fatigue, apathy at what he called the death of free cinema as we know it. It was a tragedy in his eyes and complete bewilderment in mine. I truly admired his tenacity and indignation.

Barry never blamed his longtime friend Don Selwyn. Nor did he harbor any personal resentment to the postproduction team. He knew the culprit in this debacle had been broadcast conventions, to which he would forever remain indifferent.

After Barry's public fight with the agencies he would retreat another time to his beloved west coast. He shared his time between the southwest coast of North Island and the Omapere coast line. He would write and teach. He would lecture and preach his concept of Fourth Cinema. His health would also begin a slow descent due to hypertension and fatigue. He wasn't tired of traveling or fighting, but years of devotion and dedication were finally taking a toll. One day I received an e-mail from our mutual friend Vanessa Rare, telling me Barry had had a stroke, his first. He asked her to contact me because he needed a lecture assistant in Leeds, England, in a few months. He was sure that he would be fully recovered by then.

Three months later I boarded a plane to England. After a seven-hour flight and three-hour train ride, I walked into a former castle converted into a bed and breakfast on a hill in Leeds. "Yes, Professor Barclay is awaiting your arrival, Mr. Bear." Barry was regal in his quaint sarong, sitting with a cup of tea that seemed fitted for his hands. "Kia Ora bro"—a term he rarely used. "How was your flight?" Always more concerned about me than himself, he looked frail. "It happened while I was changing bloody cords under my desk." He laughed recalling that he may have lost a book and half of a screenplay on the computer while anticipating my first question and steering, as a director does, the conversation in his direction.

It was surreal to see my friend walking with a cane. But he was as sharp as a double-edged knife, his wit deft and even craftier than usual. Barry was in his element and loved the attention paid to him by Dr. Stuart Murray's lovely assistants. The English department at the University of Leeds had been teaching a course in its master's program about Barry and his work; Dr. Murray was writing "the book." Barry was treated like a rock star, and I was his North American "red" Indian friend. It was a great visit, and despite his disability Barry danced like a poet in paradise. He beamed with pride when the concierge greeted him as "Professor Barclay."

In 2006 Barry was fêted by the Dreamspeaker festival in Alberta, Canada, where he was acknowledged with a best documentary award. At the festival he was also inducted into the Walk of Fame, and his hands were imprinted in cement. He always said that recognition by indigenous people meant more to him than anything. I was the only one who saw the tear in his eyes. He stopped in Vancouver on his way back to Aotearoa to spend some days with us. It was a glorious visit. He was happy with a new and committed relationship back in the home country. He was going home to write a book, perhaps another screenplay. By this time the cane he had used since his stroke was just a sidekick, part of his new entourage.

"Where is your friend?" he asked one afternoon after we had opened a bottle of red wine. By that question he meant my camera. "I've a few notions I'd like to get off my chest," he said. We moved to the room where I had my camera set up. Putting a microphone on my friend, I conducted our final interview, though I did not expect it to be that. He wanted to talk about the "goddamn bloody tyranny of the cutaway." That day Barry was in fine form, no signs of slowing down and all signs of full recovery from his stroke. He performed for me yet again. He rallied on for an hour about Iwi (Māori) control of their images.

Later, during the winter, I received an exuberant e-mail from Barry, telling us he had been "bonked" by the Queen. It would distract him for a while, he feared, and he wondered if he should perhaps not accept the Queen's Birthday Honours list to become part of the Order of New Zealand. "Ludicrous!" I replied. "Take the bonk!" And he did and we all applauded, laughed, and cried. It was a moment no one expected from a man who protested on the steps of the New Zealand government buildings in the early 1990s.

Barry Barclay became a Member of the Order of New Zealand in 2007, the year that would be his last on earth. That was a great year for him. He was planning another trip to Canada to deliver a keynote speech at a conference in Kelowna, British Columbia. He would write about Fourth Cinema and how he managed to remove the pistol on the table. We had plans to spend a week together. I was in final editing for a documentary that I had made from some of

our interviews and trips together when news arrived of his sudden passing early the next year. I was saddened but I celebrated his life in my tribute turned eulogy.

In Canada we continue to celebrate Barry's achievements, and he is respected by many of the first wave of indigenous cinema storytellers. When he passed away in February 2008, we were putting the final touches on our series *Storytellers in Motion, 1–39*, and we dedicated the last two programs to him and decided to end the series. There were more stories to tell, to be sure, but our emphasis on nurturing a dialogue about the indigenous voice in cinema and television was pervasive. The views of Barry Barclay inspired us to believe in our ability to create, produce, and transmit the stories of our people, by our people and in our own image.

Bazz, as he was known by friends, will never be replaced in our world and in my lifetime. He was old school, and the walls of that school are no longer made. He spoke in such an excited manner that one always felt a bit anxious. We never had a chance to say goodbye and maybe that's because we believed that we would be eternal, invincible, and somehow immortalized by our work. That's why I am not sad or nostalgic about my friend, my brother. Barry Barclay was not the prophet. He was a humanitarian, an intellectual, and someone who loved a good yarn. I miss him, and it has been my honor to write the foreword to this edition of *Our Own Image.*

Our Own Image

Author's Note

After twenty years of working in film, I made my first cinema feature during 1986. It was called *Ngati* and was set in a rural Maori community in the late 1940s. To our great surprise, the film won some critical acclaim abroad and I found myself travelling to a number of international film festivals, sometimes on my own and sometimes with producer John O'Shea, writer and associate producer Tama Poata, and lead actor Wi Kuki Kaa. After screenings we were called upon to chat informally to the audience. Without exception, people were friendly and supportive. Nevertheless, some of these sessions were a little traumatic – at least for me – because, among the queries we were up there on our feet having to field, there were frequently quite probing questions on the role of indigenous communicators working within a majority culture. I felt very naked at times: there were no research notes to refer to, no papers I was aware of from which we could pluck quotes. We had only our own experience in communications and politics in our own country to draw upon.

This small book grew from those talks. I came back home from one trip and said to myself "I'll put this down on paper before it slips away." But the driving energy to stick at the keys came from our days with Leonard George and his video- and film-maker friends in Vancouver.

Leonard is the son of the late Chief Dan George, who is remembered internationally for his performances in such films as *Little Big Man*. Wi Kuki and I sat in his family home on the reservation on the shores of the bay watching videos the local community had made. A group of youngsters swam out to the nets and brought back two live salmon as gifts, and later we strolled up dusty drives to sit on neighbours' steps and chat in the late sun.

Over the days of hearing talk from the Indian film and video community in Vancouver we felt the quiet pride in their achievements. But

we felt the pain too: the limited access to funding; the problems involved when presenting projects to panels controlled by the majority culture; the lack of respect for their languages. My own overriding emotion was one of elation – "My God, we are not alone!"

I feel privileged to be able to return these pages in memory of those days.

*Letter to the Chief Dan George Memorial Foundation,
Vancouver*

Dear Friends,
These pages are meant as a gift to the people who looked after Wi Kuki
Kaa and myself while we were on your ancestral lands in October
1987.

How do indigenous people use the camera once they come to have
some control over it? Perhaps it is on our own shoulders to rework the
well-established rules – adopting here, modifying there – so that the
way of creating images slowly becomes a little more comfortable for
our cultures.

In New Zealand we have worked to form a national organisation of
Maori communicators. It is called Te Manu Aute. A key part of Te
Manu Aute's constitution reads:

> Every culture has a right and a responsibility to present its own culture
> to its own people. That responsibility is so fundamental it cannot be left
> in the hands of outsiders, nor be usurped by them.
>
> Furthermore, any culture living closely with another ought to have
> regular opportunities to express itself to that other culture in ways that
> are true to its own values and needs.

While those principles might be straightforward enough, it has been
surprising to meet resistance to them from some parts of our industry.
We have encountered a mixture of condescension and anger. We have
had much support too and for that I am rather proud of the progress
our industry has made in the past few years.

Having achieved a reasonable climate in which to operate, our next
problem has been to find ways to adapt the technology to suit our own
purposes, and that is what these pages are about. The thoughts that
follow come from many people, but I will put them down in my own
way. I hope they will be useful.

1

A Fitting Companion

Over the years the camera becomes like a friend, something you learn to take with pride into places of great power and the humblest of villages. Yet which of us is not anxious walking with a friend into a new world? Will your friend be relaxed in strange company? Perhaps some unwitting breach of manners will spoil the occasion? The Maori world has its own ways of talking and listening, its own humour, its own process of censure and support. How can we take that maverick yet fond friend of ours – the camera – into the Maori community and be confident it will act with dignity?

Maori people are said to talk in circles. Outsiders say such talk is imprecise and time-wasting. It is not, of course. It allows many perspectives to surface, and to die too, should the substance not be appropriate at the time. There is a feeling that you have had a chance to hear everybody's voice, and nobody can complain that there was no opportunity to voice his or her mind. This process is used not just for idle things, but for debates of great consequence – debates on land matters, for instance, or fishing rights. A debate on fishing rights in New Zealand among just one tribe could well involve an area of sea equivalent to the entire coastal resource of countries such as Belgium or the Netherlands.

As a Maori technician, the film-maker is faced with the challenge of how to respect this age-old process of discussion and decision-making while using the technology within a climate which so often demands precision and answers. For instance, a documentary synopsis is expected to lay out a clear thesis in as few words as possible.

"What is your point?"

"The point is that it is not my point at all. I wish to record and present what the people think."

"Then what is your target audience?"

When you reply, "The target audience is the people," you get the sort of look a headmaster shoots at a cheeky pupil. But important talk is in front of the whole people, never in committee, never between two people in private. Talk comes of age only when it is presented to all the people.

In my own documentaries I have tried to include a tapestry of people, partly because I was fortunate enough to get a grounding in the craft amongst Pakeha film-makers familiar with the British documentary tradition, who drew on and developed that tradition in New Zealand – people like Tony Williams, Ian John, John O'Shea, Simon Reece, Rick Spurway and a host of others. I have found that grounding invaluable when working in the Maori world where the old people must have an opportunity to talk, and the youngsters too. The bankers and accountants, the farm labourers and the road workers – they all have voices.

Let's imagine you are making a film about a pollution problem in a long-settled bay. Your researcher will have boned up on the scientific side and will have a couple of articulate scientists in tow. You say to the researcher and the crew, "We are going to film the kuia (women elders) first and we are going to spend a whole day doing it." The crew is anxious to get on with the "proper" filming, thinking that reminiscences in Maori from an old woman will not find their way into the final edit anyway. Then you film the kids at the school and the rough young men who do most of the fishing in the bay. It is only towards the end of the shoot that you get the outside scientists in.

By this time the crew is likely to think the director is bananas, but for the Maori this is the natural way of going about things. The young people will not talk before the old people have been given an opportunity to have their say. Nobody will talk in any depth if they see the outside expert wheeled in early on in the piece. In plain financial terms, respect for the traditional approach can at times bring real benefits to a production. Three years ago I directed a 50-minute documentary (*Te Urewera*) for Television New Zealand as part of their series on national parks. Five weeks' shooting per programme was budgeted for, and two weeks' pre-production was allocated for each programme.

I asked for six weeks' pre-production for my programme, as I wished our team to spend time with the old people explaining the import of

the programme and getting their commitment. Having got that commitment, I felt we would then have the whole community behind us and would be able to shoot the programme very efficiently. As a trade-off, I guaranteed to shoot the programme in three weeks, rather than five. We actually shot the programme in twelve days. It turned out to be no more expensive than other programmes in the series (and cheaper than some), yet included material that has almost never been recorded on film among the Tuhoe people before, such as the old women talking about the plants used for fertility and menstruation.

It was not always easy to build up a tapestry of people during the *Te Urewera* shoot. During pre-production we instinctively put most effort into getting the co-operation of the most prestigious elders – and rightly so. In this particular tribal area (Tuhoe) the elders have rarely allowed their voices or faces to be recorded. We did get the support of the old people, but it was a last-minute scramble to get the younger ones included – the hunters aged between 30 and 50, and the women with growing families.

On some documentaries I have directed, the crew has felt that once the "guns" were interviewed, the film was in the can. They found it hard to accept that the speech from a group of inarticulate youngsters on a cold afternoon down some muddy track was vital in the effort to present the whole people, to achieve on screen that sense of community participation in important talk that is the heart of the culture.

One of the more vivid memories I have of trying to urge a crew into filming minor characters has to do with filming people in groups. People who have never been interviewed are often afraid of the camera. The technique of sitting an individual under lights in front of a close camera is disconcerting for anybody, let alone the so-called inarticulate. So why not film that person amongst the family? Why not have the kids sitting in, and the grannie? It does make more work for the crew; there are many focus points to mark up, and the lighting is more difficult. The crew may feel the extra work is not warranted because we are there to record only one key person and they will ask, "Why can't we just interview her on her own?"

I came to leave a production over this matter. A BBC crew was in New Zealand making a documentary on the Maori situation. I was

employed on liaison and helped to introduce the team into the Maori community, thinking it an opportunity to get some of the issues out into the wider world. But I was astonished when the producer flatly refused to allow the friends of Ngoi Pewhairangi to sit with her while she was being interviewed. Ngoi was one of the most inspirational leaders of her generation and quite capable of holding her own in any forum, but she wanted her friends with her – only two or three, but it was understood that Ngoi would be the sole spokesperson.

The producer became angry when I explained the situation. "We have come to interview Ngoi. Organise it." Ngoi spoke in the end, and when I asked her later why she had gone ahead with it, she simply assured me that the old people knew when they were being ripped off and how to act in response. The BBC got token, shallow words. Ngoi pulled the wool over their eyes. I was unable to explain to the producer what had happened, and why, and I took my leave the next morning, seconds before I would have been sacked.

While I believe passionately that our films should be guided by that respect for community which is our heritage, I do not believe in sloppy directing. Simply squirting a camera in every direction in the hope of finding a film in due course is, to me, a sign of a director without backbone. Films have to be cast. They should present a rich cast, one that gives a glimpse of the many-sided nature of a living community. The director must be rigorous in selecting the key cast on location, not leaving the casting until a messy collage of people arrives on the editing bench. Nor do I think it good enough to have no personal point of view, arguing that your job is to provide a platform from which the people have an opportunity to talk. That is not how "gatherings of people" are called. Similarly, a director must have vision when calling a "gathering on film".

Maori gatherings are called hui. The quality of the hui is determined by the quality of the voice that is calling the hui. Then it is determined by the quality of the response to that voice – who comes, and what they are prepared to talk about. You have to be a brave person to call a hui. Your credibility is on the line in a most personal way. Is the issue important? Do you really have the authority to draw in people of standing to talk the issue through? And will the wider community just

smile at the effort once the hui is over? To my mind, making a film amongst your own people is like calling a hui. It takes guts to stand up and say, "This matter is important and I want you to participate."

Some time ago, Eruera Nia of Te Atiawa made a series of document-aries on the rivers in his tribal area. At stake was a treaty we call here the Treaty of Waitangi, which has been invoked many times by elders and activists alike in respect to land ownership and control over fishing resources. But the Treaty also covers rivers, large and small. Was the river ever deeded by Maori to the Crown? It is an important issue; the right to take shingle from the river could be worth many thousands of dollars to tribes right across the country. So in setting out to make a documentary series on this subject, Eruera might be thought of as a man calling a hui, and that involved a bloody-minded conviction that there was a need to call a hui and a confidence that he was capable of drawing a response from the people.

Any worthwhile film involves a certain arrogance – the arrogance to call a hui, especially as a young person (under 50). If you are not brave enough to call a hui, you do not have much right to be handling the extraordinary resources it takes to make a film. Then again, the process involves humility, the humility to bend the technology to the rules of the hui – to allow the people, the whole people, to speak.

I think Pakeha people have a different sense of hui. They seem to fashion the process to "statement", to "information", to "clear format", to "agenda", to "target audience", to "objective reporting", to "spokes-persons". A Pakeha film-maker once told me something though, some-thing that has given me confidence when approaching my documentary work as hui. According to his outlook, shooting on location is like taking field notes. The thesis is written later, back at home, from the notes taken in the field. The notes have to be good, but they are not the finished study. I go along with that. I do not see it as an excuse to be sloppy in the casting or as an excuse not to have a vision before you begin shooting. I do see it as a release from a dreadful Pakeha tendency to script before calling the hui.

But "hui on film" will never be popular with everyone. I had a galling experience over a series of six 50-minute documentaries I directed for television in the early 1970s. The series, called *Tangata Whenua*, was

popular, perhaps because for the first time the camera was being taken into places only Maori go. The series is still pertinent and being screened in schools and throughout the community.

The annual television awards came around. I have little time for competitive awards as such, but because of the historic importance of the series to the country in general and to Maori people in particular, I felt the judges owed it to all New Zealanders to pay some tribute to the series. That same year, a Television New Zealand team had made a two-part documentary series in Papua New Guinea, which was just about to gain its independence. When I saw the programmes, I wondered about the tone – yet again a white interviewer was asking the black man how he was going to manage his own country now that he had got it back.

The Papua New Guinea programme carried the main documentary prize. There was a certain irony in that, because they showed the white man talking about the natives, while the *Tangata Whenua* series showed the natives talking about their own lives. We shrugged it off as one of those quirks of life, but the judges' words giving the reason for rejecting the *Tangata Whenua* series: "The series raised more questions than it answered," still ring in my ears. I would have thought that was something to be proud of. That is exactly what hui is about – having the arrogance to raise more questions before the whole people and then having the humility to let the debate progress from there.

To be any sort of Maori, you have to be a listener. You do not interrupt a person who is talking, no matter how humble that person may be – the rules about that are quite firm when formal talk is in progress. But a similar spirit is maintained even at informal occasions, such as a meal among relations, or chatting over a beer at the hotel. The liveliness of Pakeha groups, on the other hand, seems based on thrusting yourself forward, of butting in to keep the conversation sparkling, or going one better. Often enough a speaker will not even get an opportunity to finish a sentence. I also enjoy that sort of talk with such groups, but it is alien to Maori ways of exchanging thoughts. That system makes for vigorous linear debate, whereas Maori debate tends to be cyclic.

The Pakeha linear style is reflected in much Pakeha film-making where the argument is thrust forward with punch and assertiveness.

Viewers will say, "I never felt lost, I knew exactly where I was going." Nothing could be further from what Maori people will say after spending some time talking to the old people or to friends.

"What did you do for the afternoon?"

"Oh, I just sat and talked to Aunty Roimata."

"What about?"

"Well . . . this and that."

One of the great glories of Maori life is that love of contact through talk. People will drive the length of the country to be present at hui. There will be some important issue at stake probably, but between the formal discussions there will be time to sit on the steps of the meeting house, absorbing the conversations and contributing to them. People do not "feel lost" on these occasions, but neither do they know "exactly where they are going".

It can be difficult to put a finger on techniques that might better capture such a spirit when the system is based on linear talk and linear presentation. For instance, I think one of the most damaging attitudes to the free-flow of Maori conversation on film is the industry's attitude to the "talking head". For the life of me, I cannot think of anything more beautiful than the human face talking from the heart. In the Maori community, at every level, those moments of talk are regarded as the most precious of jewels. On the other hand, I can understand why producers and audiences dislike the talking head. It is because real people are turned into puppets with moving lips. There is no sense of a human talking intimately to other humans, only an image of somebody turned into a mouthpiece for the purpose of the linear argument.

Perhaps the challenge is to seek out techniques that can put people back on the screen. I believe one of the first steps is to get rid of the camera. To quote a German film-maker, Rolf Haedrich, who worked with us in New Zealand, "We are making a film, get rid of that camera."

On my documentaries we have used the long zoom lens a great deal, and more recently we have turned to the 300mm and 600mm lenses, which can put the camera 15 to 50 metres from the subject. We have organised simple, inexpensive sound rigs so that the cameraman, director and, when needed, a translator, can hear the

conversation from a distance. The only people around the interview spot are the interviewees themselves and the interviewer. The crew is invisible and people are left free to chat.

We have found a slating microphone, far removed from the interview spot, a useful device. When the director feels it is time to slate (end-slate), the camera swings across to the distant mike and the assistant slates there, out of earshot and out of the eyeline of those being interviewed. Such a procedure takes co-ordination amongst the crew, because the sound recordist will have to make the slating mike live when the time comes to take the slate. This can be done with hand signals, or if there has been time to put together a slightly more sophisticated sound rig, by a voice cue through the director's mike and the assistant's headphones.

It is important that the recordist runs sound all the time, whether the camera is running or not. It is usually possible to make magazine changes without having to interrupt the conversation, which means you can let the conversation run without having to approach those being recorded to say: "Wait a minute, we have to load more film". You need something like three fully-loaded magazines before the start of a major conversation.

End-slating can be a useful system too, especially when used in combination with an out-of-sight microphone. Slating with a clapper board still has a certain Hollywood mystique about it – two hands thrust the blackboard in front of the lens, "Mark it!" Bang! "Eighty-two. Take two. Action". The purpose of this flashy activity is to set a clear synchronisation point on both picture and sound within each shot, a point which will be used later in the editing room to bring the picture and sound rolls into exact alignment. From a technical point of view, the slate could be inserted at any time during the shot, but you can imagine the sort of life-threatening response from a director who, slap in the middle of a delicate interview, sees the assistant cameraman suddenly thrust a slate in front of the lens. Normal practice, therefore, is to slate either right at the beginning of the shot ("front-slate") or, on rare occasions, at the end ("end-slate").

Front-slating is a pretty violent affair. The camera gets set, sound rolls, camera rolls – "slate" – and because expensive film is running

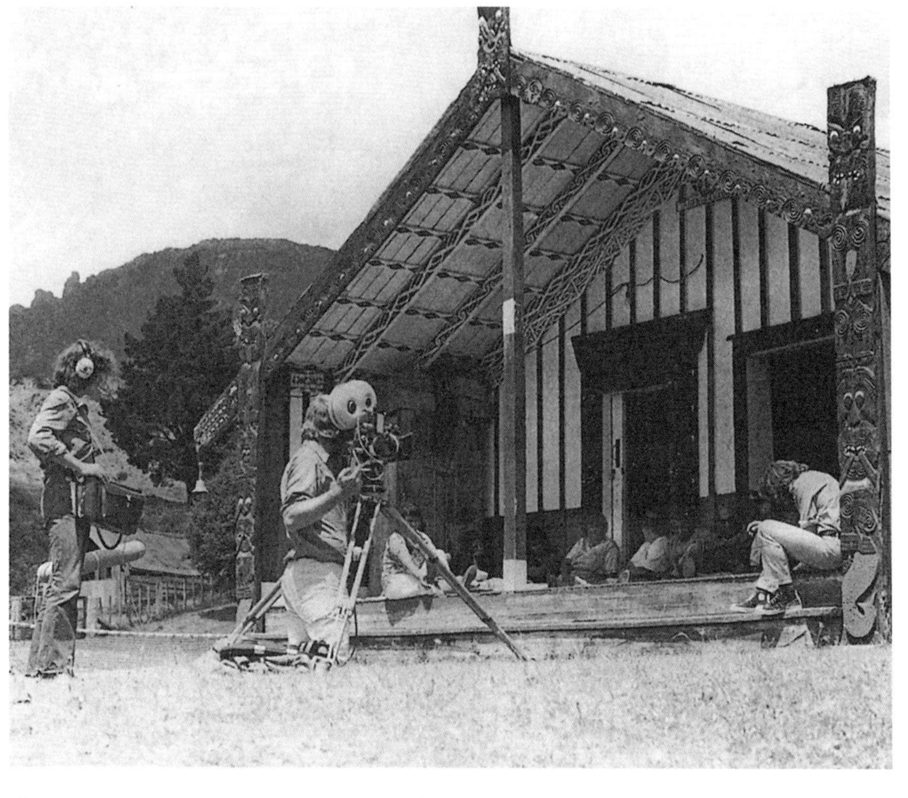

The *Tangata Whenua* crew film in front of the Takahirangi meeting house at Maungapohatu in 1973. (Left to right: Craig McLeod (sound), Keith Hawke (camera), and camera assistant Peter Jones.) It was this crew that helped develop many of the technical attitudes and procedures the author has described.

Pacific Films

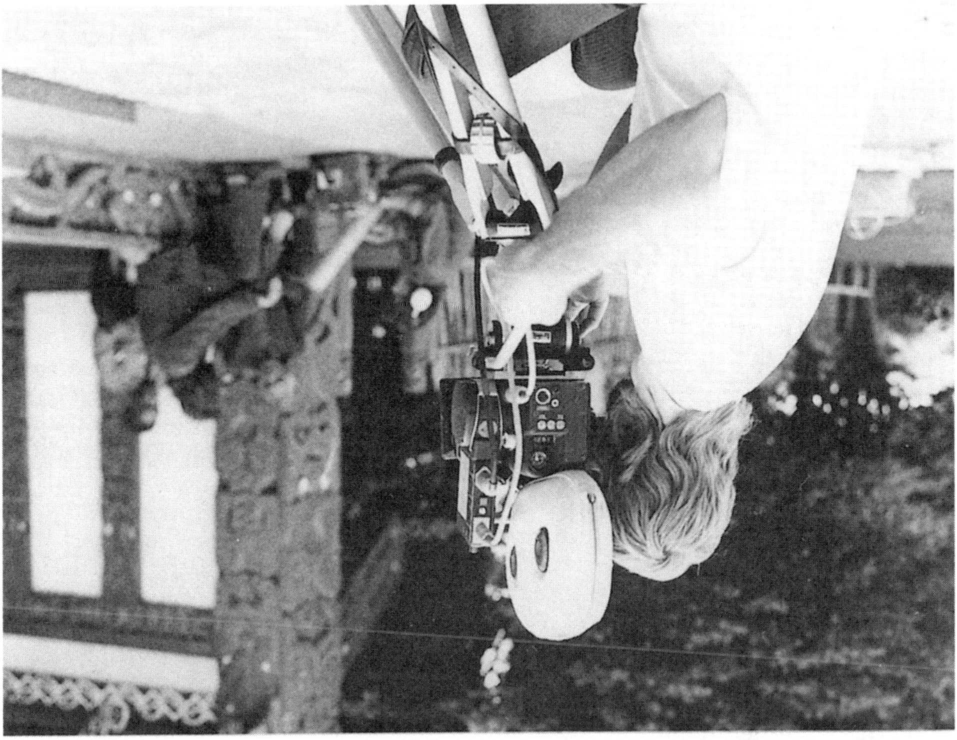

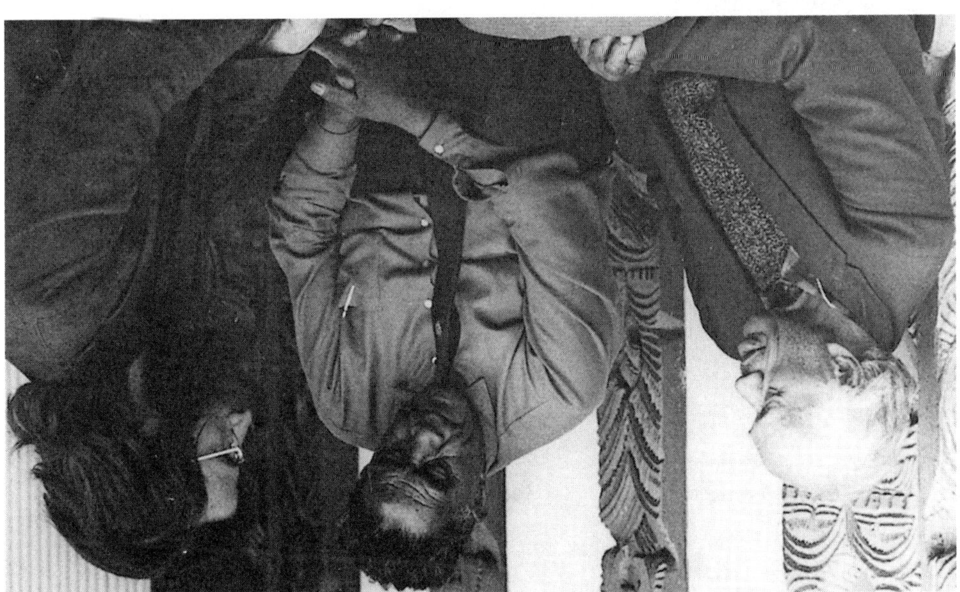

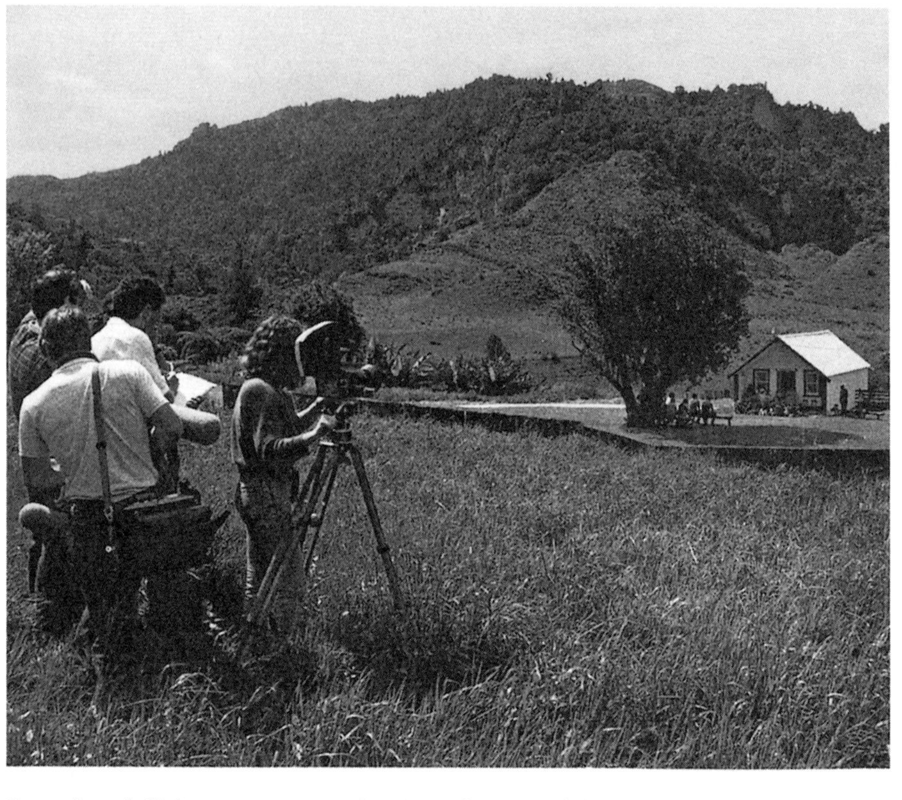

For a decade Television New Zealand's *Koha* team delivered around 22 15-minute magazine programmes on Maori topics for general audiences each year. The photograph (1987) shows a crew filming at Pipiriki on the Wanganui River for *Koha*'s five-part *Papakainga* series.

TVNZ Ltd, Maori Programmes Department

OPPOSITE: Master carver Piri Poutapu chats with *Tangata Whenua* series writer/ interviewer Michael King and Waikato elder and facilitator Te Uira Manihera on the porch of Mahinarangi meeting house, Turangawaewae marae, Ngaruawahia, in 1972. Note that cameraman Keith Hawke has the camera some 10 metres from the people on the porch, leaving them as free as possible from the paraphernalia of film-making.

Pacific Films

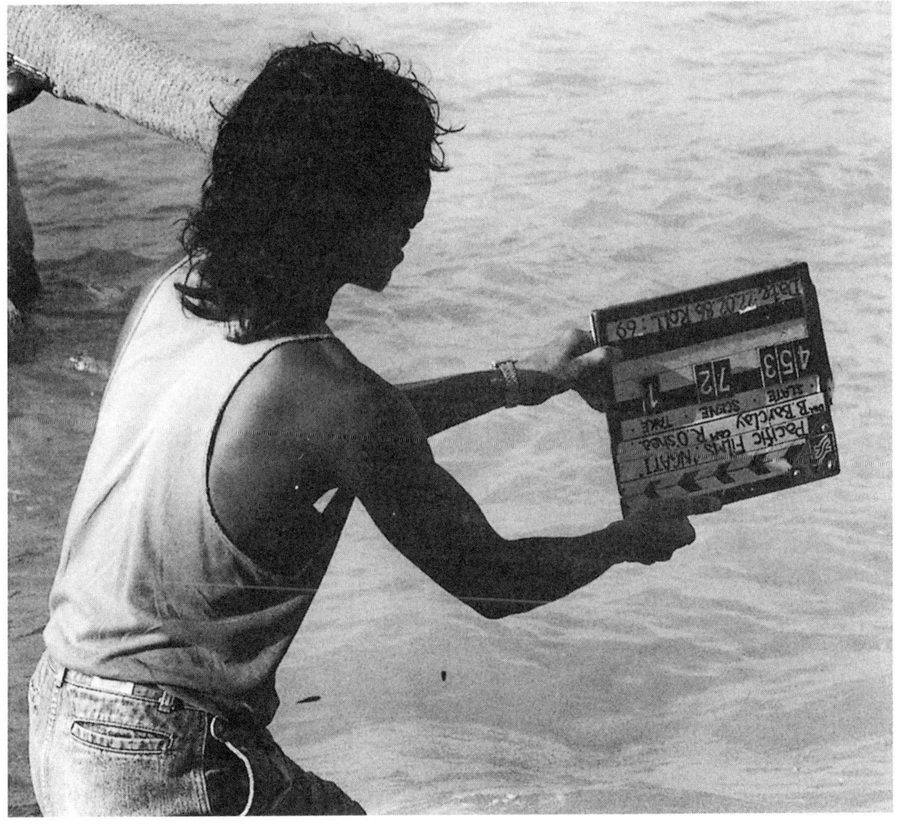

Clapper/loader Nathan Spooner slates during the shooting of the feature film *Ngati* (1986). The slate board carries some basic but vital information for both the laboratory and the editing team – camera roll number, date of shooting, scene number and the shot/take number, which in this case was 453, Take 1. Nathan is holding the slate board upside down to show that the take is being slated at the *end* of the shot (ie "end-slated")

Pacific Films, John Miller

through the camera right away, the interviewer launches into the first question immediately. It is a standard procedure, but it produces talking heads.

End-slating (especially when the slate is being recorded out of sight on a slating mike) means that the important talk does not have to start right away. The subjects can chat about whatever they like. When in due course the talk swings round to the substance of what the film is about, the camera can be flicked on. When the conversation drifts off the subject or becomes repetitive, the camera can quietly swing away to take an end-slate without interrupting the natural flow of the conversation. Some editors can be silly about end-slates, maintaining that they are time-consuming when it comes to synchronising rushes. That is balderdash. The trick is to synchronise from the end of the roll, and for the director to make sure all the slates are end-slates.

I usually allow up to half a day for a conversational interview of the kind described, much of which will be spent rigging up and doing the normal PR work. The actual talk, in my experience, may take anything from 40 to 90 minutes. I would allow up to 1000 16mm feet of stock, but some can be got on 400 feet. The system is tough on the crew, as it requires them to hold positions right through the 90-minute shoot; ready to turn on at a couple of seconds' notice. The cameraman has to keep an eye to the eyepiece, following the subjects with all the precision of one actually shooting, which can be very draining, at times creating hostility because the crew might feel: "Why the hell can't the interviewer get on and ask the relevant questions?"

The system is tough on the director too. You have to make instant decisions about when the camera should be turned off and on, knowing that you cannot allow yourself to move in and say to the subjects, "Could you just repeat that piece? I'm not sure we got it properly." Meantime, the footage counter shows that the dollars are clicking by.

I believe we might do well to further explore how to make the camera a listener. As a Maori, you are taught to be a listener; you sit at the feet and open your ears. You have no "right to know". The knowledge is gifted to you at appropriate times and in appropriate places. Those

who do not have the patience and the humility to undergo this way of learning are unlikely to ever gain much of real depth.

It is not easy for some to accept being a listener. I have seen people leave formal Maori gatherings on the point of tears or fuming with anger. "We made an effort to come here to learn things, and all you people are doing is talking around the point." Sadly, such people (and they make up a fair proportion of the population) are never going to gain any insight into Maori ways. As the years go by, the camera is coming to be more freely invited into the Maori community, and I suppose it is up to us as technicians to make sure our friend behaves in a fitting way. All too often it struts like a young person who wants to get to the main point immediately. A camera of that kind is wont to pace here and there, attempting to hype things up like a vain bird during mating rituals.

But the camera can act with dignity at a hui. There is a certain restraint, a feeling of being comfortable with sitting back a little and listening. Of course what I have arrogantly called strutting has its time and place too. The track and the crane are part and parcel of the film-maker's basic tool kit, and well used, can produce breathtaking results. On the other hand, it is all to easy to indulge the tools and lose that sense of modesty that is considered becoming at hui.

2

The Other Eye

In our country we have the phenomenon of the spa pool, and it is nice to attend a party beside one, with light wines, smoked cheese, and a collection of actors, writers, directors, designers and a technician or two. "Bitching", "back-biting" and "slagging others off" are part of the fun amongst such groups, and healthy too, inasmuch as the worries voiced usually come from a care about our chosen craft.

But let us suppose some Maori film-maker moves in next door and stages a party around his spa pool. The talk around the Pakeha spa pool is likely to be mixed about the brown crowd over the fence. "How come they got to get a spa pool? Look at all the help they get. We have to struggle for what we have." You know the kind of thing. But if it is a good brown spa pool, there is sure to be some lively talk going on, talk meant for Maori ears only. It makes one somewhat cross when, late in the afternoon, the people from the Pakeha spa pool are looking over the fence, a little astonished, a little scandalised. "We went to all the trouble of making sure they could have a spa pool of their own, and all they do is argue among themselves." They retire to their squares of cheese and the brittle talk that is the juice of show business anywhere in the world, hurt that the noble savage is not turning out quite as they expected. Within the Pakeha industry, when people have uncertainties and squabbles, it is called healthy debate. When the Pakeha see the fledgling Maori industry going through the same uncertainties and squabbles, they talk of an inability to get along.

It is a fearful thing, that face watching across the fence that rings your spa pool, that eye that seems to know how you should talk over your smoked cheese, what shape your projects should take, and indeed what posture you should assume in the drawing room – an instant recordist, a committed protestor, or a person exploring what are delightfully called "Maori values".

Paul Holmes, a long-time friend and one of the country's top radio and television personalities, wanted to interview me at 8.30 am for his show. He was kind enough to telephone me the night before and run over the questions he had in mind. One of the things he wanted to ask me was whether *Ngati* (a feature film I directed in 1987) was a Maori film. Thank heavens I had the night to think it over.

During the interview I told Paul that I thought a Maori film was a film made by Maori, just as a New Zealand film (in contrast to a French or Dutch film) was one made by New Zealanders. Simple enough. However, I added, perhaps a hidden question was being asked, one that is not usually asked of film-makers from the majority culture – whether *Ngati* really had special values underpinning it – Maori values that were somewhat different and more meritorious than those one could find in any other of the 80-odd feature films made by New Zealanders in this country since 1930. It is as if you have to prove to the majority culture that your project will be genuinely Maori (in the eyes of the majority culture) before you can gain support to make a Maori film. Perhaps women in the industry have a similar problem; they might feel they have to prove a point to the industry, which is so dominated by males, that their project is genuinely from a woman's viewpoint.

As I see it, a woman's film is one made by women. A Maori film is one made by Maori. A Maori film might be very violent, or frivolous. Maori films might deal with incest, robbery, or love under the apple tree – who is to say? A Maori film might have nothing whatsoever to do with what both Maori and Pakeha are pleased to think of as "the Maori style of life" – communal attitudes, a respect for the elders, a love of the land.

For the majority culture, marital break-ups, murder, the law courts, domestic violence, the generation gap – all this is the very stuff that keeps the wheels of their drama industry turning over. But to float a Maori film, you can feel you have to float Maori values, whatever they might be. We shall get to know what a Maori film is when we get a chance to make more films, just as the majority culture here, having now made a substantial body of work, can review its efforts and reflect on the way it has created images of our country. It would have taken

a brave person to stand up ten years ago to define a New Zealand feature film. Nobody was asked to do that. I sometimes feel we are being asked to do it as an unspoken condition for getting support.

Perhaps that is why I got so cross at a panel session in Vancouver, when a young Canadian, doing his best to be helpful, suggested that maybe we would have more success with our scripts if we based them on a policy of positive imaging. Mr Shakespeare did not have to worry about positive imaging – look at all the crooks he wrote about. Mr and Mrs Macbeth, for example. I am not sure that we could make a brown *Macbeth* here at the moment, because such work would not be "Maori". To be fair, some of the resistance would come from within the Maori community itself. For me, that is simply a mark of how deep the oppression has been.

I have a dream. I want to make a Maori kung fu movie. I think a proposal to make an exciting Maori kung fu would create hostility in almost every quarter, Maori and Pakeha, liberal and conservative – and that is exactly why one part of me wants to do it. Before the arrival of the musket, the Maori world had a rich tradition in the martial arts. For instance, the use of the taiaha (a traditional fighting staff) was every bit as scientific as the things Bruce Lee wielded. Taiaha training was tough and each move had its name. How good it would be if kids could go down to the video parlour and get out a film called *The Taiaha Kid* instead of a kung fu film from Hong Kong.

I fear the script of *The Taiaha Kid* might be too impious for some of the assessors. It would not be a worthy Maori film. It would not reflect real Maori values. The funny thing is that a good proportion of the films the country has turned out in recent times do involve kung fu-type events – bridges collapse, cars rocket in flames down cliffs, the police cars skid out of control. Perhaps these scenes reflect real Pakeha values, I don't know. What I do know is that the producers and directors who put forward these projects and got them funded did not have to explain the cultural values underpinning the script. And I am pretty certain that if one tabled *The Taiaha Kid*, one would have a little talking to do.

I served time on a good panel here, one that makes grants for people who want to do something innovative on film or video. The grants are

small, but they are targeted at projects which are likely to stimulate new directions either in an individual's work or in the industry. About 80 applications a year come into this fund. The fund has made some bold stands over the years, supporting projects that were off-beat or politically unsavoury at the time. I was amazed to see how many of the applications had to do with alienation from the land.

Applicants are encouraged to submit sample work on film or video. Going by the sample work, students in their third year at art school who apply to the fund – the Arts Council Creative Film and Video Fund – seem to have a fixation about their feet. I have seen their feet walking on tarmac, on black sand, on tussock, on carpet, and on pedestrian crossings. It seems that one's own feet walking on a pedestrian crossing is one of the supreme images of alienation from the land.

We coined a word. Being a neat and tidy liberal panel we were naturally against anything that smacked of racism or sexism, and after watching so many feet, we agreed we were against "landism" too. The coined word is a nonsense. It just helped us to express our frustration about feet that could not find their place on the land on which their owners were born.

Maori people too are mindful of where their feet stand. Identifying with your tribal land is fundamental to a Maori person because the land gives you your turangawaewae ("the place where the feet stand"), your identity. Many dispossessed Maori search with anxiety for that one plot of soil they can claim as their turangawaewae. Yet it seems to me that that sort of anxiety is very different from the feelings of alienation espressed through art school images of drifting feet. Tarmac or tussock, it is –for Maori people – ancestral land, no matter what the current government might say. Dispossession, yes; alienation, never. The drifting feet syndrome is a Pakeha phenomenon, along with ageism, suburban neurosis and marathon-running in middle age.

The Pakeha community takes such subjects for granted. It is quite normal for its youngsters in their formative years to express these sentiments of alienation which, it seems to me, you have to be rich to dwell on at all. Indeed, I suspect that many Pakeha like to see themes such as alienation surface in the work of those in their late teens, thus

reassuring an older generation that their children are beginning to grasp the real facts of life in a world it has perceived as being too big and wide and cold. An organisation making grants for script development has little trouble handling applications for films on alienated feet. It can be a different matter when an idea comes in from a culture that has no sense of being an alien on the land.

From time to time we have got wind of one or two simple projects that, by rights, should have come to the Creative Film and Video Fund. For instance, one Maori group in Taranaki wanted to record on video tape an elder walking the land around those marae in Taranaki running kohanga reo (language nests), nurseries for pre-school children in which the Maori language is taught. The idea was to have an elder talk in good but basic Maori about the names of the river, the mountain and other sacred spots adjacent to the marae. The recordings would then be used as a teaching aid in the kohanga reo. But this idea has not yet made it to the fund because those whose idea it is are finding it hard to enter the contest arena, competing for funds against what look to them to be more sophisticated ideas.

It is to be hoped that this project and others like it will eventually make it to the fund. The panel is an excellent one and would welcome such projects. From the applicants' point of view, however, it looks more like a Pakeha arts fund from which students get funds to film their feet. The tragedy of the matter is that the people who have steered the fund along over many years – particularly Roger Horrocks, if I might single out one person among many – are wholeheartedly dedicated to supporting projects which are rooted in the real needs of the community. Indeed, the fund has given money to new Maori communicators on a very generous basis.

The lesson for me in this is that many Maori are intimidated by the climate which has been put in place by the majority culture. They are afraid even to articulate their idea outside their immediate circle, for fear it will appear childish when compared with the ideas educated students at art college come up with. In other words, on top of all the normal nervousness you have when faced with that blank page on which you must set the first word, you have the problem of setting your words out knowing that what you are writing about may not look

sufficiently sophisticated to those who are going to scrutinise it. I am not talking about the flow of the words, about literacy as such, but about the concepts behind the words. You feel you do not have the right clothes to go to the Pakeha party, even when people are waiting to welcome you at the door.

All this would change perhaps if the panel were Maori. The applicants would know that they were presenting their ideas to people who knew how important is it to be able to name your own river and mountain. The applicants would also know that the sun might not automatically shine on an application from a relatively rich city-based arts student. If major panels were Maori-controlled from time to time, surely all New Zealanders, whatever their ethnic background, would gain much from having to present their ideas to a different mentality. Maori panels for general funds are not likely to be created, of course, so the temptation then is to argue for a portion of the general funding to be placed under Maori jurisdiction.

We have had mixed experiences with such Maori funds. They tend to be under-funded in comparison with their Pakeha counterparts; they are the first to be cut back in bad times; they tend to introduce a ghetto factor as far as Maori artists are concerned; and they have the effect of closing off the major fund to Maori, who no matter what the scale or nature of their project, are steered to the Maori fund.

And Maori administrators can suddenly become better Pakeha than the Pakeha. For some years a group of senior Maori women artists has been running its own non-profit-making collective which has had a number of major successes, reported on very favourably in the Pakeha press. Yet the women have encountered such chauvinism from some parts of the Maori arts fraternity that they have chosen to withdraw from the main Maori arts organisations, preferring to rely on their own networks for support.

For these reasons we have firmly resisted splitting our major film funding sources here into general and Maori. But that means we have to reconcile ourselves to the fact that those assessing Maori scripts will not be riding the same set of mental rails.

There is uncertainty amongst the fledgling Maori film and video-making community. We lack technicians. We lack depth of experience

in preparing and presenting projects. After years of being treated as a poor relation, many have a bitter distrust of the Pakeha industry – sometimes, I feel, to our own cost.

Most of the Maori film and video-makers have come from television or from gaps in the independent industry. I do not feel equipped to comment in any depth on what it has been like for Maori writers, presenters and producers who have developed their skills within the television system. I have worked on contract to television from time to time, but I have not formally had to clock in for a 9 a.m. start within television. Still, looking at it from the outside, one winces at what some of our friends have had to go through over the years – low budgets, poor technical back-up, and lack of access to prime time. In the last couple of years some major changes have been attempted within the television system and we can only wait to see whether Maori within television will get an opportunity to develop their skills in a more congenial climate. For many of those who began making films outside the television system, the spark came from major here-and-now protest struggles. Bingo. We have the protestor image.

You will be familiar with this pattern. A major issue crops up – the occupation of a piece of tribal land, for instance. Someone with an interest in the camera will grab whatever equipment he or she can lay hands on. Some spare stock is found, a couple of lights are given free by friends, and shooting begins. To my mind, such people are special for two reasons. Not only do they have a capacity to spot the symbolic value of what is happening way before most of us have even begun to hear what is in the wind, but also, as a director, I feel for them in that they, like any communicator, are removed from the action, if for no other reason than they are so busy twiddling knobs that they mightn't even have time to fling a fist in the air before being arrested.

After the initial flurry of activity, the film-maker is soon forced to look for funding to continue the shoot and start the edit. The funding, usually meagre in the extreme, will come from the system in dribs and drabs, from state sources and from the churches and other voluntary groups. Although I don't want to demean the efforts of groups that raise money for "minorities" in times of crisis, at considerable cost to themselves, perhaps by running fund-raising screenings or by dipping

into their own slim project resources – may such goodwill continue in our country – I am nevertheless cynical about the system's support for film projects of this kind. Such support tends to reinforce the image of the minority film-maker as a valiant artist beating on the outer gates of a comfortable system which, whether liberal or conservative, is rather pleased to have a little protest. And it is convenient for the system to be able to view the committed Maori film-maker as some dedicated sod prepared to have the telephone and electricity cut off for non-payment in order to film other committed Maori being led off to prison in a good cause. It is important that such films be made, but I resent the way some of my friends have been cast in this mould by the majority culture. What about the little animation film? A brown soapy? A *Taiaha Kid* ?

It has been interesting to see how European people follow the pattern. For some years I lived in Europe and worked with various European groups that fund "struggles" – efforts to get clean water to villages in Eritrea perhaps, or basic reading materials to children in Malawi. At that time, I had hopes that we could look offshore for funding to assist in making films about the situation at home. It was a desperation measure, because at the time New Zealand funding sources had little interest in Maori projects of any kind. We had no success at all.

In particular, I recall a discussion with a Dutch group, NOVIB, the largest non-government aid agency in Holland, funded partly by churches and partly by the government. I was with Maori film director Merata Mita. We did our best to explain the Maori situation – how Maori are, after the aboriginal peoples of Australia, the most-jailed people in the world, how there was a hidden apartheid operating in New Zealand, and the like. The NOVIB officers spent some time explaining what we would have to do: we would have to link the issues to something that Europeans could relate to, and they cited the aboriginal campaign they were funding as a good example of how it might work.

The Europeans like to run the occasional campaign against trans-national companies, many of the major ones being based on their own soil. These companies do bad things in foreign countries, and some of what they do is especially bad to native peoples. By highlighting the

deeds of the transnationals, the campaigners said they were able to run successful education campaigns which drew media attention and gave them opportunities to raise funding. In the case of Australia, they had focused on the mining companies and their treatment of the aboriginal people, particularly in regard to aboriginal land claims. Could we think of a similar handle on which to hang the Maori situation?

It has its funny side. The new noble savage who may be shown off in the drawing rooms of the white world is encouraged to rattle, not the spear, but the camera, and the majority culture is pleased to fund one or two of them from time to time. But when you turn into a difficult native, the drawing room is likely to clear fast. For example, the Education Department generates materials specifically directed at Maori children. So does the Justice Department, the Health Department and the Housing Corporation. Why, we have asked, should these materials not be produced by our own communicators – by Maori writers, video-makers and graphics people? The drawing room empties.

The majority culture is also pleased to find the instant recordist. The pattern seems to go this way. Rewi lives in a small Maori village. He becomes inspired to do something on film or video and gets a lot of community support. He seeks advice on costs and discovers how cheap (on the surface) it is to shoot on video tape, and he finds an organisation willing to make a small production grant. He records, probably borrowing a friend's car to serve as camera vehicle, and pays himself nothing in wages. Now Rewi is faced with the edit. By this time, his budget is almost exhausted and he has to look around for more money.

People are astonished that he has not been able to complete his project on the grant he has already received. If they are going to invest further, they will want to see something of what has been shot. It is not good policy to show raw rushes, but Rewi has little option. With luck, he will get additional money, enough to cover a week's hire of an editing suite. He will probably have to edit under pressure with no time to experiment, working through the night when the editing facility is not being used by commercial clients. His programme will be crudely cut, but when he presents it to his funding sources they will be delighted enough. In fact, I have had the experience of sitting in on such screenings where the donor organisation has expressed surprise that

it had been possible to make a programme of such quality on such a low budget.

Such surprise and delight is rubbish – I have seen so many productions of this kind where just one more week's editing would have meant the difference between a tight programme and a promising home movie.

Now the pattern repeats itself for Rewi. Potential donors hear that he has made "quite a reasonable programme for a newcomer" and say they would be interested in receiving an application for his next project, naturally at similar budgetary levels. Rewi comes to believe he really is developing his communication skills. He may even come to argue against other ways of operating. If we multiply the fanciful example of Rewi 30-fold (and there must be at least 30 other young Maori in his situation) we arrive at a rather ominous scenario. When you come to jump up and down about getting more support for Maori film and video development, the authorities say, "But so and so is making wonderful tapes back in his tribal area." Or "We know of two young men in the Waikato who are recording week in, week out. They have bought a caravan and travel from hui to hui." (The last is a direct quote.) In other words, the problem is solved as far as the majority culture is concerned.

Nevertheless, there are many benefits to be gained from this kind of recording. The recordists at least gain some contact with the technology through hands-on experience. They are using the technology within their own community, rather than in the Pakeha community making, say, video clips. The community sees its own young people recording material that the community itself has thought important to record. However, for both the community and for the young communicators there are, in my opinion, dangers.

The most obvious problem is the low technical standard that is achieved on the equipment available. Broadcast-quality equipment in this country is expensive to hire and, even when some have the dollars in their back pockets to hire it, it is sometimes difficult to persuade the owners to release it to young Maori communicators with no professional background. Probably the best way to get the equipment released is to take along a trained Pakeha technician, but having a Pakeha technician accompany them is not something most young Maori

are prepared to countenance these days. Thus many projects wind up on half-inch video, with all the limitations that format imposes when you try to achieve a professional result in the edit and in duplication.

Using the technology in this fashion creates a false impression of what it really costs to make a good well-structured programme. We get cases where quite highly-placed Maori executives will suddenly want a 30-minute programme done on some Maori artist or on an employment scheme targeted at Maori people. They will set aside $NZ15,000 and expect a new programme maker to turn out something that can be used nationally and even on television. Currently there are a number of young and not-so-young communicators who are so happy to be given any sort of a role in production that they go along with such naive thinking.

Recording is not programme-making. Programme-making has to do with creating a metaphor from recordings taken in the field. The majority culture in New Zealand is quite happy to see an abundance of low-cost recording take place in the Maori community, but it is giving precious little help to those who have a desire to turn recordings into metaphors. It makes me angry to see so many of the talented newcomers trapped into accepting the recordist role graciously handed down to them by the system.

All this might change if we could set up a full video editing facility under our own control, although I am uncertain myself. Such a facility could obtain some commercial work as well as being made available to various Maori communicators at cut rates, but interest rates, maintenance costs, permanent premises and the like would probably force such a facility into running a commercial operation making company training videos, government department promotion videos and so on. Still, why not? Such a commercial operation, backed by cultural determination, could benefit the Maori community greatly. My concern is about something different, for I doubt whether the problems concerning the country-wide push to get young people to cut their teeth on "instant recording", with no realistic opportunities for "metaphor making", could be solved by a major Maori video-editing facility.

Some of our companions around the brown spa pool do not always seem to grasp just how important it is to have real control over our

own image-making. We, like you, have our Uncle Tomahawks. But we also have some incredibly dedicated people in key positions, people whose life – and I mean whole life, day and night, seven days a week – is given over to improving the situation. But even among the really dedicated people I get the feeling there is still a certain innocence about Maori control of Maori communications.

For instance, I am at a loss to explain why film- and video-making has not yet filtered into other parts of the Maori community. Perhaps it is simply a matter of growing up. Fifteen years ago the Pakeha community did not have much time for film- or video-makers either, but since then the Pakeha image industry has blossomed haphazardly by way of promotional and educational films, television commercials, documentaries and dramas, and more recently, feature films. Little of this progress was initiated by the government, the arts fraternity or the captains of industry. It is possible that we have to go through the process as well.

Within the Maori arts scene there has been a fantastic resurgence in traditional Maori arts and crafts such as carving and weaving. And there are Maori artists who are national figures in Pakeha arts like painting, drama, music composition, sculpture and writing. But so far we have not managed to centre the film and video arts within the Maori art mainstream, and from time to time I have had Pakeha people kindly explain to me why. They say that painting/writing/music are closer to the craft skills and spirituality of a tribal people who are used to making up instant poetry in their oratory, or who have developed fantastic visual skills by daubing outlines of wild animals in cave walls. Video and film, they imply, are new media to which it might take some time for an oral culture to adapt. It reminds me of the days when many New Zealanders were proud to boast that Maori men made amazing bulldozer drivers, failing to appreciate that the same men, given equal education and employment opportunities, might also be able to run a computer.

The fact that Maori communicators are not yet in the Maori arts mainstream is having real repercussions for our young film and video community. It hurts me to see our writers selling off their film and video rights to Pakeha producers. It hurts me when a Maori officer

within a government department recommends that a training film aimed at Maori youth be contracted out to a Pakeha production house. It hurts me when a senior Maori artist is happy to be profiled by a Pakeha crew, saying he is only interested in being filmed by "the best".

Maori film-makers are in a transition period. Most of the younger Pakeha film-makers have not been through anything similar. Their development, collectively, has been much more rounded. Rock video clips, alternative films at art school, working with foreign feature film crews as a grip, animation, pack shots for frozen peas, blowing up cars, television news, promotional films – these are activities that helped develop the majority culture's film-making skills. Most Maori have not had that variety of experience.

Perhaps we are over the hump. There is now an eagerness amongst Maori with some training in the craft to tackle a variety of projects. That was not so even five years ago. I was asked by Leslie Kukoloio in Hawaii when that time might come in Hawaii. "What triggers the explosion?" he asked. I said I hadn't the slightest idea; it just seemed to sprout from the ground at a certain time. It could be that film development follows other developments. As film-makers, most of us now have little compunction about standing up and saying "Don't keep lecturing us about how to make films. Give us the resources and we will do it in our own way." The boldness and determination to do that has come from a much wider struggle.

Maori control of Maori matters (or "mana motuhake", as it is called) is being pushed in the trade unions, in health care, in education, in local government, and in a host of other areas. Perhaps that general determination to be in control of one's whole destiny – and most of the active Maori film-makers in the country have been part of that wider movement in some way – has created a climate within which the film-makers feel confident enough to assert the same principles in their own industry.

3

Setting Out

The real sailor – the one with the salt in the blood – seems to me to have an odd light behind the eyes onshore, a light from a bucking and horizonless plain unknown to those of us who prefer to take our morning toast and coffee in a kitchen that does not shift. I live in a port town and sometimes see them out of place in streets that for me simply link my favourite greengrocer and butcher shops. I have sailed once or twice and have experienced the peace of seeing the harbour hills under stars take their leave astern.

A van packed with lights, tripod, lens and camera cases, clamps, wedges and other craft paraphernalia roaring a day's drive towards a gully known only to a few farmers – this also has its own mystique. Kilometre by slow kilometre the regular world slips behind and suddenly you are on location. A few weeks later, back in port, the crew swaps old stories – how a vital camera battery was left on charge back at the motel, what it was like walking down through the bush to persuade a contractor to shut off his chainsaw for two hours because the noise was making it impossible to record sound.

There will be other stories to emerge as the project is ushered through the editing rooms and the laboratory before being thrown up on the public screen for the first time – the best-loved sequence dropped, the day the producer told the investor to go jump somewhere. And when it is all over, those who put the thing together will be as restless as land-bound sailors anxious to return to blue water. It is an itch, film-making, and a cheeky business, involving the madness of a sailor in even daring to push off from the wharf. Well, our canoe has at last been pushed off. It might be somewhat leaky – but hi-de-ho!

I ran a training course, one of the first of its kind here, I guess. It was a four-week short, sharp exercise and fairly ineffective, except for its symbolic value in signalling to both Maori and Pakeha communities

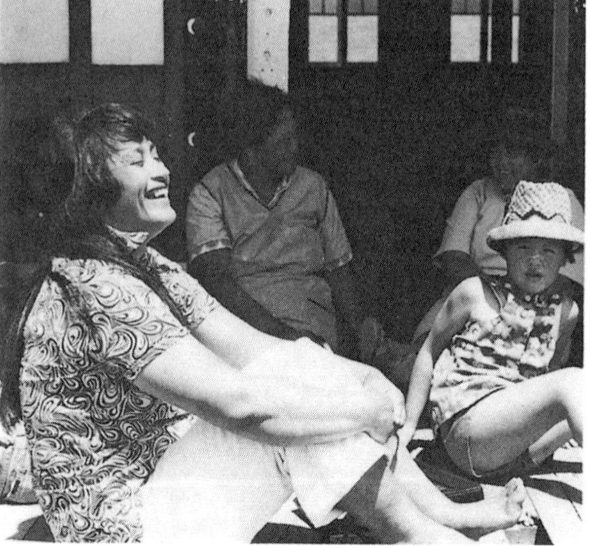

"One of the great glories of Maori life is that love of contact through talk." Wai Harawera, left, at Maunga-pohatu (1973) shares a joke during the shooting of the *Tangata Whenua* series, and below, Te Uira Manihera chats with Herepo Rongo (1972). Te Uira was one of a small band of leaders at that time who sensed the potential of the camera and helped make it possible to film in some parts of the Maori community with a frankness not previously achieved.

Pacific Films

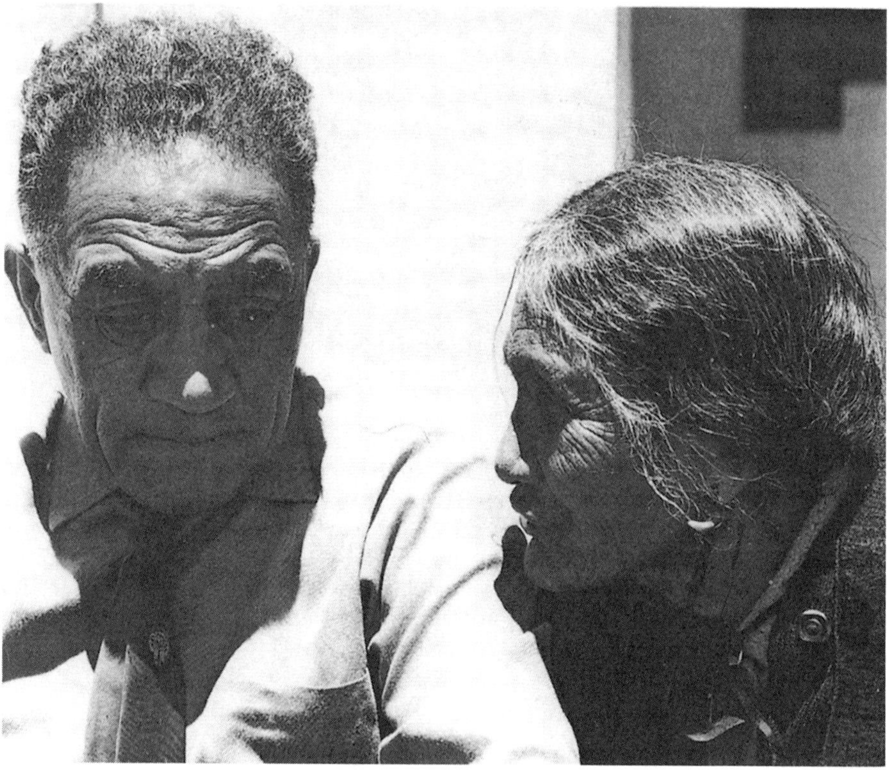

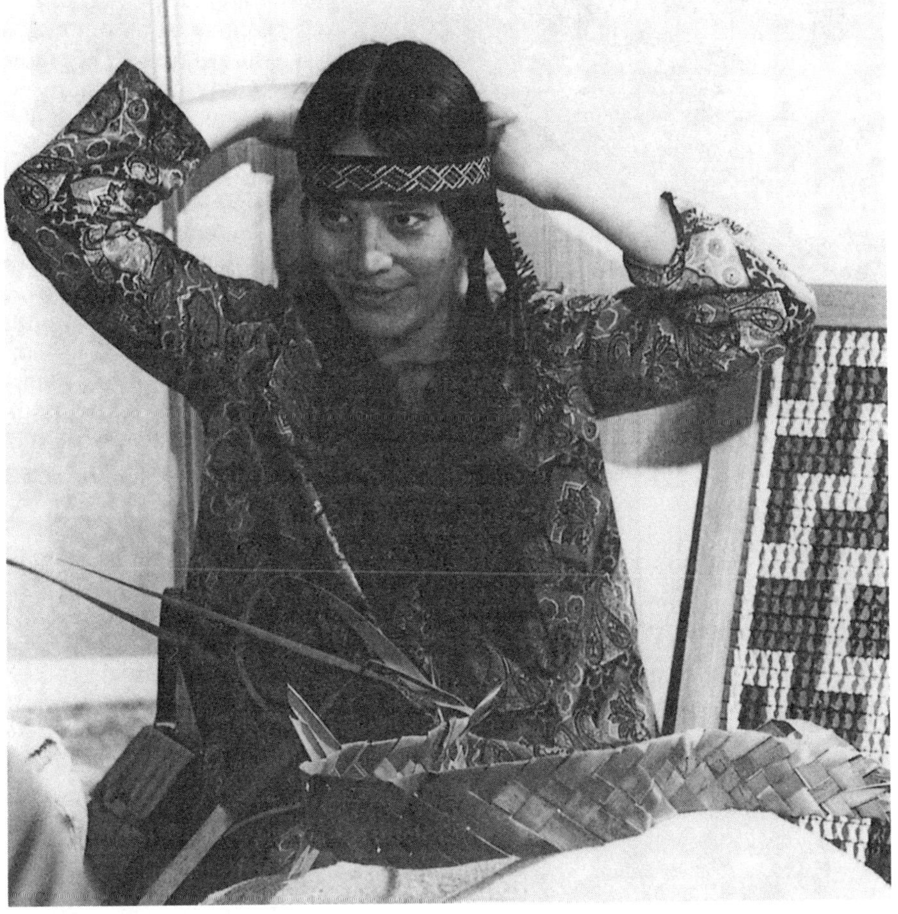

During the filming of an informal craft session for the *Tangata Whenua* series, Meretiana Davies ties on a taniko band she has completed. At that time (1973) women's traditional craft skills seemed to many to be on the point of disappearing for good. But since then – thanks largely to the work done at the community level by determined women right across the country – there has been a vigorous resergence in these crafts, a resurgence that involves women of every age. The newer crafts of film and video do not yet enjoy such a wide base in the Maori community.

Pacific Films

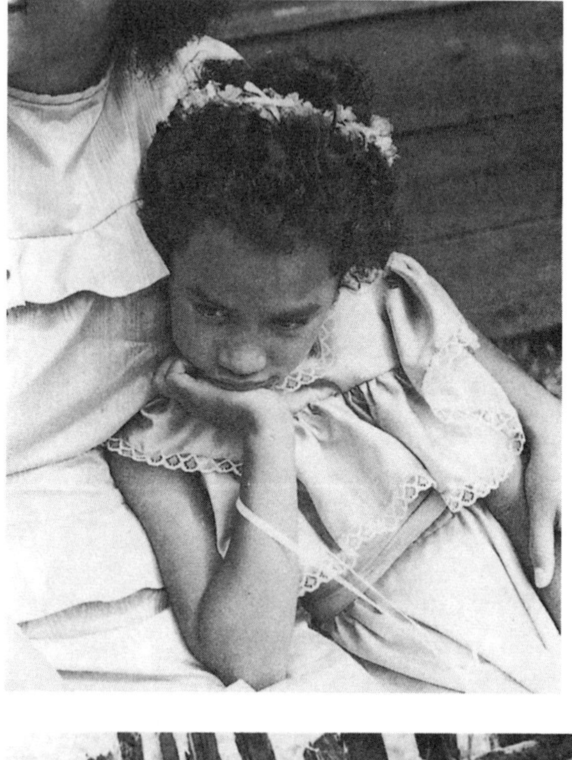

As any performer who has worked on a location drama is likely to tell you, most film-making is waiting. And so, relaxing between takes during shooting of Merata Mita's cinema feature *Mauri* (1987) are lead actress Rangimarie Delamere, left, and below, from left, Mass Campbell, Moe Kerei and Raukuna Hogg. Merata wrote, produced and directed *Mauri*, and is the first Maori woman to realise such a large film project. *Awatea Films, Vicky Ginn*

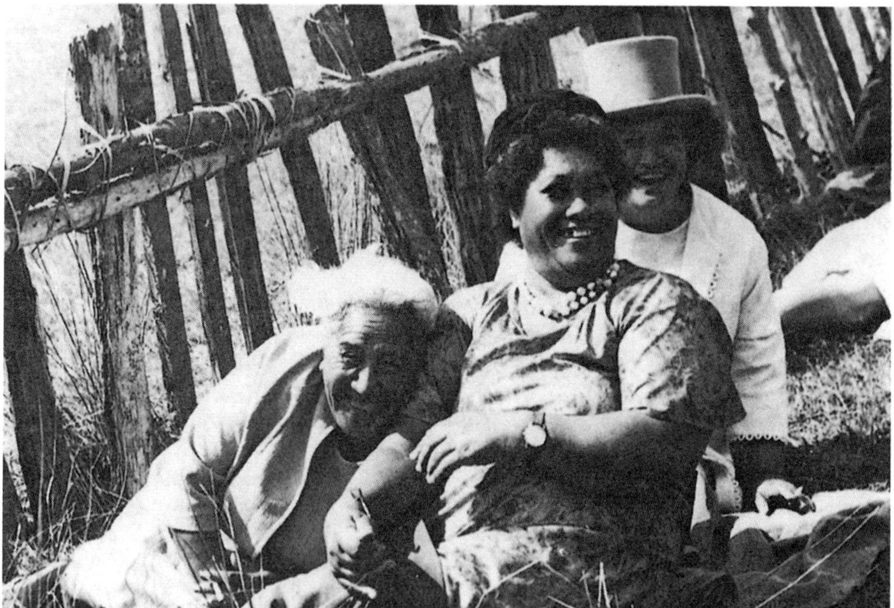

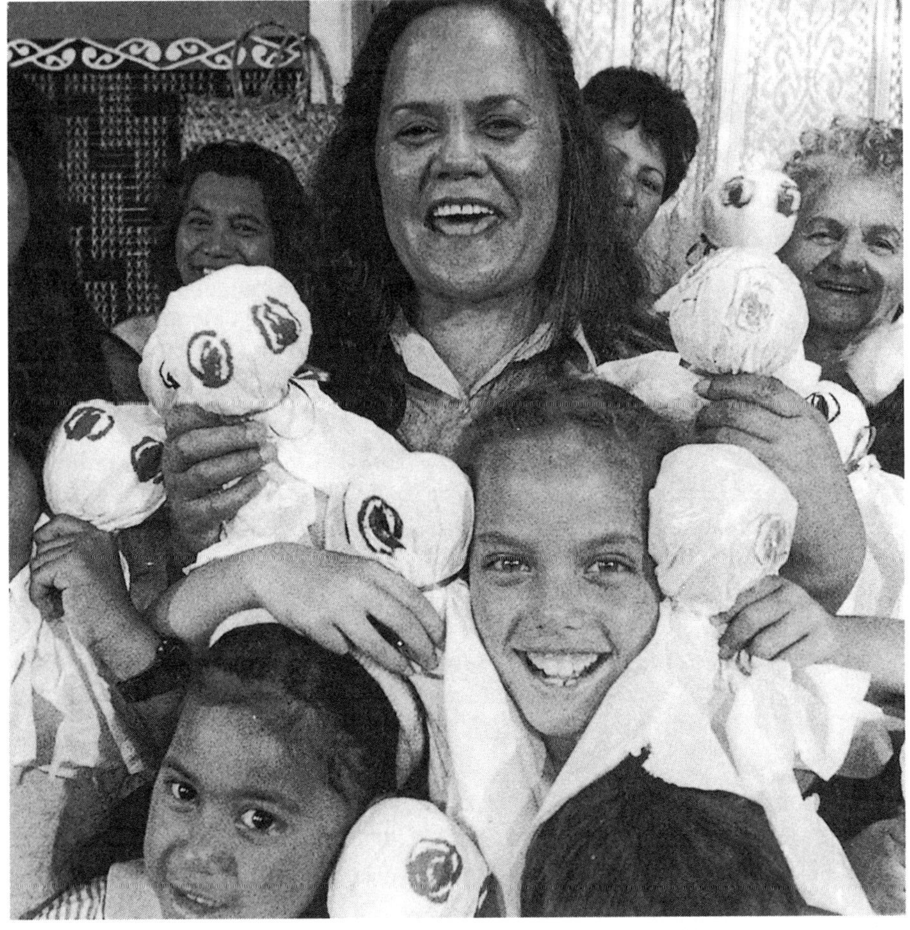

Television New Zealand's *Kohanga Reo* series was designed as a television teaching aid for the Kohanga Reo where the Maori language is taught to pre-schoolers. During 1987 and 1988, 200 10-minute programmes were transmitted. This scene (1987) was taken on Whataapaka marae on the upper reaches of the Manukau Harbour. The adults are, from left, Henrietta Maxwell, Moehau Reedy and Lu Tuhura.

TVNZ Ltd, Maori Programmes Department

that something along these lines had to be done. I was in a happy position. I came in with a good deal of money which had been granted by the New Zealand Film Commission for materials, equipment, transport and the like. The 30 trainees were to be chosen by the Labour Department and their wages – a mere NZ$10–15 a week above the dole – would be paid by the same department. I knew that any of the trainees who showed promise could move on to the crews of a half-hour drama I was about to shoot (*Kamate Kamate*) and then on to the feature film *Ngati*.

The venue for the course was the Hawke's Bay Polytechnic at Taradadale. It so happened that the college had a marae-like complex. (In general terms, a marae is a fenced-off open space with two or three buildings, which is set aside for Maori communal gatherings of many kinds.) How the marae complex came to be in that community college is a story in itself.

Hawke's Bay has a large Maori population. The administrators of the polytechnic began to wonder why it was that so few Maori enrolled in their courses. They asked a senior Maori staff member, Mana Powhiro-o-te-rangi Cracknell, to look into the matter. Mana, in consultation with the local Maori community, came up with a Maori solution to the problem. He knew there were three army-style prefabricated buildings on the fringes of the modern complex. He proposed turning the buildings into a waananga, or Maori "school of learning", assuring the administrators that Maori students would come.

Mana began organising courses on the marae – a typing course for Maori youngsters, for instance. But the polytechnic had been running a typing course for years. What was wrong with Maori students going to the long-established course? Some hostility was generated among the staff against the marae concept, and it was into this climate that we walked when we ran the film waananga.

We were in a privileged position. We had money and we were going to be there for only four weeks. Film-making had, to the regular staff, a mystery beyond typing, and film people are somewhat notorious for poking a tongue at systems, so we were given space. Nevertheless, at times we had to fight for our space. The Labour Department would not agree to a Maori-only group. That would be seen as racist, so one third

of our group was Pakeha. Lesson one: it gets tricky when you try to set up native-only programmes here.

Lesson two emerged through the programme. Despite the predominance of Maori amongst the participants, the Pakeha intake could dominate proceedings in the twinkling of an eye. For instance, we got our first batch of film back from the laboratory and we were eager to start editing it. Guess who grabbed the equipment?

When I arrived, I told the students my time was theirs, 24 hours a day, seven days a week. We would keep the school of learning open for as many hours as people wished to learn. And we did. I understand it was the only time in the history of the polytechnic that full-time students worked every weekend and right through one long holiday weekend. At times the lights would be burning at ten and eleven at night. This created problems because the cleaners moved through at 5.30 p.m. and we were not allowed to use the room after it had been cleaned. We made a deal with the cleaner, a Maori woman, assigned to our room. She had a cup of tea to serve out the half-hour assigned to her to clean our room, and we cleaned the room when we had finished, which was often late. One thing Maori groups are good at is cleaning up after a show – you are taught that very early on.

The cleaning lady was caught out by the other cleaners, who threatened to report her, so we made a new arrangement. We helped her clean the room at 5.30 p.m. and then proceeded to mess it up again making movies. Late one night, one of the security guards read the riot act to us, promising to call the police to evict us because "the room had already been cleaned". We said we were quite happy for him to call the cops, but I think he chickened out, for we did not see them.

The allocated room on the marae was numbered N748–49. We unscrewed the number plate. After all, some of our group had lived under numbers for a good part of their lives. When it was made clear to us, in no uncertain terms, that the number had to stay, we named our group Te Awa Marama, designed a logo, painted up a sign with our name and logo on it and hung it over the number. That was not taken down by anybody.

The group felt very uncomfortable about eating at the cafeteria. The food was cheap but the atmosphere was very Pakeha, as was the food.

We decided to cook for ourselves. The room we were working in had been used earlier for cooking classes, so there was an ample supply of plates, large pots and electric elements. Each day we brought in our own food and cooked it as part of the course. But cooking for ourselves got us into strife. The Labour Department said that in the weekly wages paid to its "clients" there was a daily allowance for lunch (about NZ$1.50, as I recall). Why was I providing additional food? I pointed out that the food was coming out of our general film budget granted by the New Zealand Film Commission and that catering was an important part of film production. The Labour Department then threatened to deduct the personal lunch allowance from our students' wages. We said that in that case we would guarantee to use the Labour Department's allowance to buy sandwiches at the cafeteria, but we could not guarantee that we would not feed these to the seagulls. At that, the matter was dropped, but it would have been hopeless to tell the department the real reason why none of us wished to eat in the cafeteria.

Indeed, one of the prize moments for me on the waananga came when I urged the group to come up with a subject of their own they might like to cover. A little shyly, a couple said they would like to film the cafeteria after the students had finished eating. I had no clue what they were talking about, so they took me to have a look. The cafeteria was in a small, open courtyard which had been nicely landscaped with various shrubs. In the morning, the courtyard was a picture, but by afternoon it was a pigsty, littered with half-finished sandwiches and paper bags.

It turned out that the couple who had the idea for the cafeteria sequence had been talking to the cleaning women, who said how disgusted they were at the conduct of the student nurses, all of whom were Pakeha and most of whom were from well-off homes. The woman could not understand how such well brought up girls could not even be bothered to walk five steps to drop their rubbish in the rubbish bins set up on every corner of the courtyard.

The attitude of these young Maori people comes right from the heart of the culture. You do not abuse food. You clean up. It moved me that people considered drop-outs, jailbirds and ignoramuses should be

incensed enough to make a film about the crass conduct of "civilised" students, who wore clothes they would never have the money to buy.

The food issue did not die away. The polytechnic administrators became cross because the course was meant to be a film-making course; cooking had not been scheduled on the training programme. Neither was language teaching. We had some women with toddlers. The room was big and there was space to run a nursery at one end. We would have liked to run the space as a kohanga reo (Maori language nursery), but under the rules of the college, we would have been out of line. The room had been allocated for a film course – full stop. An earlier course in the same room had run into trouble after proposing to set up a kohanga reo. It had also run into trouble because the women dared to hang out their children's nappies on a line at the back of our small marae complex.

I do not mean to be too angry. Our waananga had a lot of fun, and part of the fun was being determined enough to make our own rules. For the first time in the history of the country we had a Maori film crew operating. We forged our own environment and were proud of it.

I won't forget those four weeks quickly. They opened my eyes to what is at stake when you start to create schemes for training Maori crew. First, apart from some very supportive people in the New Zealand community, the system does not want Maori crewing, and probably never will. Maori crewing for Maori projects is about as acceptable as the idea of women crewing women's films is to most men in the established industry. What was instructive for me was to see the way the system sets up barriers.

We have in New Zealand a self-made millionaire, Sir Robert Jones, who has become a folk hero to many. Bob Jones is an outspoken man on many issues and he has firm views on what Maori ought to be doing to better their lot. Being Bob, he puts his views in pretty colourful language. Recently he appeared on a television panel debating race relations. Some Pakeha family friends winced on my behalf, thinking that some of his comments would be offensive to the Maori people. But I do not believe Bob is a racist in the way my friends think of racist. He doesn't care a fig what colour people are. But they all have to have an ability to get up and go, and for that attitude one has to

respect him. The only snag is that if we are going to get up and go, we have to get up and go in the Robert Jones manner.

The film and television industry is now keen to start including Maori technicians and are prepared to go to quite special lengths to assist in training and in making employment openings. The impulse is usually well-meant, but the hand being offered might well be like Bob Jones's hand. "We would like to see a Maori sound man", but (unspoken), "a sound man to work in the industry", meaning, working on Pakeha features and commercials, and taking on all the airs that go with that type of work.

I held a rather tense conversation a few years ago with a training officer who had been involved in television's regular training programmes for some time. I asked what policy they had towards Maori training. The officer said that, in fact, television had made efforts over the years to increase the Maori intake – they had gone out of their way to do that. I asked the officer if they had ever taken consultation from Maori people about who should go in and under what conditions. The officer said that that had not been necessary, because they had training programmes with a good record which had been in place for a long time. I pointed out that the track record was not too good for Maori, because after 26 years there was hardly a single Maori technician working for television.

"Well, they keep leaving."

Before the phone was put down on me, I managed to make one suggestion. I told the officer that what I would propose would cause laughter. I was told to go ahead with my suggestion anyway.

"A kitchen. The Maori trainees need a kitchen of their own."

The officer did laugh.

The food issue at the film course we ran at the Hawke's Bay Polytechnic was no joke at all. Cooking and eating together is a Maori thing. For an hour or two you can be Maori, away from the eyes of others. You can make your small talk, recharge the batteries, and then go back to your task in some niche within the vast complex, knowing that tucked away in other niches are other Maori, other parts of the family. When we insisted on cooking at the polytechnic, the system showed its true colours and, for the same basic reasons, I

think it might take years to get a Maori kitchen within television. It is too threatening.

Te Manu Aute's view is that Maori projects should be handled by Maori, and that means Maori technicians. Not all agree with that. Some senior Maori reporters and directors have said quite openly that they couldn't care less which technicians they worked with so long as they were proficient. The "I just want the best" syndrome.

There is a language issue too. Directors and reporters filming in the language say that it is no use having a Maori crew unless they are fluent in the language. "We might as well use Pakeha." The language requirement set by such people immediately cuts out 95 per cent of young Maori, keeps Pakeha technicians in work and potential Maori technicians on the dole. Why not include language training in the technical course, just as the language is included in the training of those Pakeha people who, in at least two government departments I know of, have the opportunity to take four hours a week on full pay to study things Maori? But generally there is now a strong push for training technicians. Merata Mita included as many Maori as she could lay hands on to help her shoot *Mauri*, as we did when shooting *Ngati*.

For three years, veteran Maori communicator, Don Selwyn – backed by Selwyn Muru, Brian Kirby and others – has been running a hands-on film and video course, *Nga Taonga I Tawhiti*, for young Maori. It is a 12-month in-depth course, run aong Maori lines and under Maori control, but enjoying a very generous input from skilled people in the Pakeha film and video community. Sixty students have graduated from this course already. Other training schemes have moved quietly ahead too. Tama Poata and Eruera Nia both have trainees in place, and there will be other community training efforts around the country that I do not know about. And in 1988 Television New Zealand brought 50 Maori into the television system for 12 months' training in a whole range of skills from floor managing to overseas marketing.

Whether all this activity will bring about immediate structural changes is doubtful. It makes one angry to know that the television training programme *Kimihia* had to be funded in part by the Maori Affairs Department. Television New Zealand provided facilities and staff time, while Maori Affairs paid the Maori trainees' wages. Pakeha

women, like Maori people, do not have reasonable access to large New Zealand institutions either, but at least when they seek entrance to them they do not have to crawl off to the Ministry of Women's Affairs for their rent and food money. Grizzles like that aside, there has been a big shift in attitudes in the last two or three years, and some people both within and without television have put their necks on the line to make them happen.

Te Manu Aute's attitude to Maori training is that the only really effective climate in which to train Maori people is where Maori are trained by other Maori, in a Maori environment, on Maori projects, and with the explicit expectation of being able to work on Maori projects in the future. Each of these elements is important. For instance, previous Maori training programmes have resulted in Maori being shunted off to the other end of the country to work on sports programmes. That was, and still is, a deliberate policy. The thinking is that we shall train you for the overall system, and just because you are Maori does not mean you will automatically have opportunities to work on Maori programmes. You take your place in the roster queue along with the rest. Maori become disheartened and leave. My own position is that I will travel anywhere to help train Maori technicians, but not for sports programmes.

I made training a condition for my accepting the offer to direct the *Te Urewera* documentary. I happened to have a very sympathetic producer, Neil Harraway, who had had little contact with Maori communities before. He came with a fresh mind. I asked to take on some trainees from the area (Tuhoe) for the duration of the pre-production and the shoot, and I undertook to raise funding for their wages, travel and food. Neil agreed. I also asked that any trained Maori within television ought to be made available for the shoot as a matter of principle. There were only two who would have been suitable for that particular project: Ru Rakena and Wayne Leonard, both trained sound-men. Neil went into battle on our behalf and I have great admiration for his tenacity, and for his anger when the bid failed.

The tussle with the various heads of department within television went on for three months. It so happened that our request came right at the time Television New Zealand was seeking to integrate its video

and film sound recording sections, an exercise made touchy by union concerns. The two men I wanted were ticketed for video sound recording but not for film sound recording. It did not matter that one of the men had run a sound department (location and studio) for a major Australian television channel. It did not matter that one had boom-operated on a New Zealand feature film. There seemed to be no way to get round the ticketing issue. A video recordist is a video recordist, a film recordist is a film recordist, and never the two shall meet.

Neil found out that there were television funds set aside to retrain video sound recordists to qualify as film sound recordists. As well as the normal wage and location allowances, the trainees were eligible for training funds on top. It would have meant that my Maori sound-man would have had a handsome sum in the hand for the three weeks' shoot, training for a job he could have done in the first year of his seven-year career. But it all came through too late. By the time the relevant heads had agreed, the two men had been rostered on to filming the Pope, because every technician available was needed to cover that prestigious visit. So while we filmed Maori people in the Urewera, they covered the visit of the Pope.

It made me hopping mad that the system could not see the value of having a Maori sound-man on the crew. Had I been doing an alpine film I would have been able to call on any technician who had experience on mountains, Pope or no Pope. The same would apply to any film to do with underwater work or blue-water sailing. Safety is at stake on those kinds of projects. But another kind of safety is involved when entering a traditional Maori area, and just as you are very choosy about who you hang off a rock with at 7000 feet, I am very choosy about whom I go on to a marae with.

I have mentioned the instant-recordist trap that video technology might represent for the paddlers of the new canoe, but nevertheless video must open up exciting possibilities for Maori communicators. For example, video recording makes it possible to place the copyright of the sound and the image in the hands of the tribe without delay. Instant replay on location means that the tribe physically sees what it

owns. Furthermore, picture and sound masters can be returned intact to the tribe, whereas with film the masters are normally best left stored in the film laboratory and in some sound studio far off in the city.

I have to leave it to others to explore just what horizons are opened up to a tribal people by having the kind of copyright control video offers. I suspect the implications are profound. For instance, certain knowledge in the Maori world is considered tapu, or sacred, and such knowledge may be very specific not only to one tribe, but to a single family within a tribe. I would be very hesitant to record such material on film, because I know from first-hand experience how hard it is to guarantee that the circulation of the knowledge gifted will always be in accordance with the wishes of those who passed on the knowledge in the first place.

The first national Te Manu Aute hui was held on Takitimu marae, Wairoa, in October 1986. Eruera Nia recorded portions of the weekend because he saw it as an important event in the evolution of Maori communications. When the last farewells were over and we were all dying to set out on the long drive back to our city bases, Eruera set up his video camera and spent three hours taping the most senior elder on the marae, the last man, so the local people told us, who knew the history of the marae in great depth. When shooting finished, he passed the tapes to the old man. They were for his use and that of his immediate family.

While Eruera and his crew were recording, I spent the afternoon kicking my heels. Everyone else had gone. I was tired after two and a half days of sometimes steamy debating. I could see that I would be arriving home at dawn after an all-night drive in the camera van. But then I saw the tapes being handed over. In 20 years of working with film I had never been able to make such a gesture to the local people.

In September 1987 the Maori community held the first-ever national hui on Aids. Along with a lot of other major health problems, Aids is not discussed openly in the general Maori community. Like lung cancer or poor diet, it is a known hazard "out there". The public information programmes on Aids in New Zealand have been as intensive and effective as such programmes probably can be, but they have been Pakeha-generated and have not touched the Maori community much.

Hence, the national hui on Aids was a most important event, a time to bring this issue out in public for the first time, and to do it in a way that was traditionally Maori.

With only a week's notice, the two Maori organising the hui turned to Eruera Nia to record the two-day gathering. They scrambled to get enough money together to hire a broadcast-standard video camera and to buy tape. Eruera recorded about six hours of the hui, hoping to edit the speeches down to a one-hour package and to circulate copies to marae and Maori community groups around the country.

There is a reluctance on the part of the majority culture to see the value – the psychological value – of hui. The material shot at the Aids hui is seen as being no different from the home movie-type recordings of umpteen hui that have been recorded – on Maori crafts, or a weekend spent discussing traditional fishing rights. "We're not going to put hundreds of dollars into editing up to six hours of a couple of days on a bloody marae."

In this particular case, the hui-type presentation was exactly what would be effective for a Maori audience, who would see their own people speaking in a marae context about the unspeakable. Such a sight would strike the Maori heart much more deeply than any pamphlets turned out by the Health Department.

Yet the video tool brings with it its own problems for those of us trying to drive the canoe beyond the harbour hills. The production ground to a halt in the edit. I suppose if our friends had been working on film we might have been able to pull off a trick or two. With an unscrupulous determination to get something out of the issue, we could have argued for a film production grant of NZ$15,000 – even $20,000 – which would have been proposed as the first third of a budget towards a short educational film on Aids directed specifically at the Maori community. This would have been a "hot" film project idea for the kind of funding sources we have in New Zealand. One can get that kind of money within a week if the matter is pressing – hence the virtue of a hui which will never be repeated, happening "next weekend". You might have to rough out a list of other sequences, which you can do happily enough, knowing in your own mind that it is unlikely you will ever shoot all of them.

To get the hui recorded on film, with processing, sound transfers etc (i.e. up to the point of editing), would be possible for $10,000, but we would have gone for $15–20,000 anyway. To give you some perspective on costs in New Zealand: a professional 50-minute documentary for television can be made from between $100–150,000. Six independent half-hour Maori dramas have just been completed to a scheduled budget of $150,000 each. A low-budget 16mm "cause" documentary of 50 minutes could, with a lot of volunteer assistance, be made for $60,000.

So you shoot the hui, process the film, transfer the sound, produce a workprint and then go to ground. The glamour of film should have attracted just enough funding to get you through editing the material in your own back yard. Within four weeks or so, you have an edited product that can be taken back to the original grant organisation for top-up funds (if indeed extra funds are required). If these tactics sound devious, be assured they are, but it is a deviousness that is forgiven by the system here, provided good material comes out in due course.

Our friends who launched off on the video trail were not able to employ these tactics. Rightly or wrongly, nobody wants to know about a $15–20,000 grant to record a weekend hui on tape, no matter what the issue. And certainly nobody wants to know about six hours of unedited tape after the event.

There is another set of shackles that can disadvantage both Maori and Pakeha communicators whose talent steers them towards video production. It has to do with the flow of money. For most projects, but by no means all, it is pretty well established that film and video production – taken to the point of release – cost about the same. But when the costs occur differs, depending on whether one is working on film or video. Let us break a production budget up into an arbitrary set of equal units – say ten units. In a film production, five units will be used up by the time editing is ready to start. Those five units will cover pre-production, purchase of raw stock, crew costs on location, and processing etc, to the point where the editor is able to begin cutting. And let's say one unit will be needed to complete the edit, leaving four units for final laboratory printing costs and sales. That makes a ratio of 5:1:4.

In a video production covering the same topic, the ratio will be rather different. The first component will be lower, say four units. The second component will be much higher than film, say four units, leaving two units for wrap-up transfers, duplications and sales – a ration of 4:4:2. The difference between the two ratios is very important; it affects the tactics. If you are going to launch off on a production, you need at least enough money to get the material back to the editing room. In the case of film, five units are needed. Video is cheaper to this point (four units). To get the material edited, only one unit is needed for a film project, whereas four are needed for a video edit. That is the crunch. Your funds on a video production can run out at just the wrong time. Last year one five-part video documentary series and one 50-minute documentary were bogged down in the editing room. Because even one hour in the video editing studio is so expensive, the directors were trapped (and still are) with a half-finished edit that is in no shape to screen to potential backers.

Obviously film productions are just as likely to come unstuck as video productions, but with film you have more low-cost options. If things get really rough, you can buy up or borrow simple editing equipment and edit the film in a spare space in the living room of your house. You can take whatever amount of editing time you need to achieve the impact you are after, with little more than the cost of the electricity to run the machine.

All that having been said, video has so much to offer the paddler of the canoe, and many young people are starting to make use of this way of collecting images.

A seed sprouted within Kahungungu, the tribal area where we ran the polytcchnic film course. The result is technically rough, but it is one of the more moving video productions I have sat through. The project was made by a group of young Kahungunu women and Te Awa Marama, the group we formed at the film course.

The women were campaigning against incest in the Maori community. It is not easy for young Maori women to stand up in public and confront their elders on an issue such as this. The video drama is in two parts: the first part comes from the early times. The greatest woman who ever lived in those times was Hine-Nui-Te-Po, and because

of a disgrace in her background, she removed herself to the world of night where she remains as a guardian, guide and final authority. When our time comes to die, Hine-Nui-Te-Po will be there to usher us through. The first part of the programme told the creation story and Hine-Nui-Te-Po's place in it. The second part of the story is contemporary. A young woman is abused by a relative and suffers the same confusion that befell Hine-Nui-Te-Po. In the finale of the programme, the situations of the two women are tied together. The blend of the two histories makes a proud statement and the resulting video is an incredibly effective tool for the kind of campaign these women are running. The video will never get to any international festival, but what those women in Kahungunu did reminds one that films and videos come from a passion. If the passion is there, the technology and the finance will fall into place, training programmes or no training programmes, kitchen or no kitchen.

Late in 1987 we approached a respected boys' college in Wellington to ask whether it would be possible to establish a Maori video unit within the college. The thinking behind this approach was to set a precedent that would have implications for the whole country.

The fashion today within colleges is for computer equipment, but five years ago it was for video equipment. I think it is fair to say that the equipment often arrived before the teachers could handle it; within a school there would be one enthusiast who would lobby the headmaster, much like kids pressing for toys they have seen on the latest advertisements on television. The climate being what it was at that time, the teachers were given the equipment, but often it disappeared under their own wing – but not in all cases, for some teachers have done some stunning work with students.

In the case of this particular college the teacher who controlled the equipment ruled that students who wished to make use of it had to join the college's video club. A teacher's pet situation grew up: to get into the club, students had to have some of their own video equipment at home. This ruling immediately excluded a large number of students, and particularly disadvantaged Maori students whose parents were generally not as well-heeled as Pakeha parents. Meantime the video club regularly used the equipment to record the college's Saturday

rugby matches as a record for the college, which has a proud rugby tradition.

I do not mean to be harsh on teachers who have acquired equipment for their college, and who put a lot of spare time into seeing that it is being used by at least some pupils. A physical education tutor or a piano teacher will also have a favourite group and give a lot of personal time to them. Nevertheless, some of us think it important to change practices within schools because, for potential Maori communicators, that is where the communications rot sets in.

We put our proposal to the college for a Maori unit which would work on Maori things themselves, rather than operating through the existing video club and filming rock and rugby. We undertook to secure a grant for tapes and sundry costs. It was all approved, though with some trepidation. Of course, there was an awkward barb on the hook – the unit must be Maori, and be free to work on a Maori project. That is called bringing in a system of apartheid (as if one didn't exist already). You will know the usual obstacles: "We have a significant Greek community. I am sure the Greek students would like to record their grandfathers too. How many units can we have?"

When asked what a suitable subject might be, we suggested the Maori unit might film Maori in the area talking about the area. It so happens that the college is situated on some of the most historic Maori settlement areas in the lower North Island. Why not get the local Maori community to explain the background of these sites whose history stretches back hundreds of years? The kids had to face a rocky road, and the project never really got off the ground.

Some of the bumps along the way came from the college itself; the teacher supervising the students' time wanted evidence that they really were doing research as they claimed. He wanted to know how much time they had spent at the National Library and wanted to see notes and photocopied articles. I had instilled into them the determination to go nowhere near any library, but to go to the people. It seems the teacher found it hard to accept such an approach. The break-up of the college year and some personality conflicts within the young group new to "show biz" ended the attempt. Hi-de-ho!

Merata Mita ran a video training course for a bunch of young kids in Auckland, where she lives. They were off the street and rather tough, but they became proficient at handling the equipment, and could put a sequence together. In due course, Merata told them they were on their own. They were to go out and shoot something and she was not going to show her face until it was finished. She gave them only one piece of advice: "Don't go imitating Hollywood. Shoot something you know about."

Three months later Merata received a phone call from the group: they had finished their video and could she come and have a look at it? She asked them if they were really sure they had finished it, and they said they were sure. The location was good – a street at night. The acting was real – the dart across the street to the alley, the climbing up the side of the wall. The material was well-structured – the close shot of the feet on the roof; the hands lifting up the skylight; the anxious face. Merata watched, thinking, "This is so real." Then she sat up in her seat. Not only did it look real, it was real. The kids had filmed one of their break-ins. When Merata hinted that maybe this was not such a wise choice of subject, they said, "Well, you told us to film something we know about." They were proud of their work – they had had to jump through the skylight three times to get the camera angle right. What's more, the cops had not caught them. Merata had to admit it was very accomplished video-making, even though the programme will not, for obvious reasons, get a wide release!

4

A Pen Among Strangers

The roots of the foreign script climate run very deep. Take the verse from the Bible:

> Be fruitful, and multiply, and replenish the earth, and subdue it; and have dominion over the fish of the sea, and over the fowl of the air, and over every living thing that moveth upon the earth.

If a script based on that principle were submitted to a Maori panel, it is likely it would be rejected straight off because, from a Maori point of view, the command is fascist, if those among you who are Christians will forgive me for saying so. It represents a blank cheque for screwing the earth for human purposes. It may be a good directive for the human race, but where does it leave the forest and the fish? Maori thinking over the centuries has never been that way, is not now and, I hope, never will be. Yet it is my impression that it is one of the precepts that underpins so many films made by the majority culture.

Just think how many Pakeha plots have do with "having dominion over". It could be the big-muscled lad "confronting the wild" to build a log cabin with his axe; or somebody taking on the system and achieving success by beating it, no matter what the wreckage along the way; it could be the man conquering the woman; or the country kid making it in the city. None of these have much to do with Maori values, which teach that to conquer is of little use unless you have moved in companionship with the people and fought your battles without the expectation of a crown.

In the Pakeha climate, cruel things can happen to the outlook of Maori communicators. I have sat through chats with one or two of our senior writers who have insisted that the hero plot, the conqueror's plot, is the real stuff of drama. There have to be winners and losers in a real drama, they say. I do not blame them. The industry has been

flying in foreigners to tell New Zealanders how to write scripts, and it seems these foreigners have all read Genesis.

Some of us get seduced. Say you sense that the "have dominion over" directive in Genesis is starting to catch up with the majority culture. You see that the forests are being drastically depleted, and that the general community is starting to get worried about this. You mention in passing that the Maori world has intricate tribal rules to make sure such a thing never happens. Ears prick up. Couldn't such values be presented within a film? You feel yourself being tempted, you drop in an extra couple of lines here, a little cameo there. In effect, you are stroking the hand of a friend-for-one-night, and even though you know you are doing it, it is tempting to continue. The relevance to one's own community is almost nil.

Take something as simple as a beach. Maori rarely sunbathe. They go to the beach to collect seafood or to fish. Yet for the film mythology of the majority culture, the beach is a playground. Couples go there to be wanton or to discover some innocent Eden between the water and the land. At times a lonely person will go there to end it all. I find it hard to recall more than a couple of films in which I have seen an individual, a couple or a family go to the seashore in the way that Maori do – to collect seafood.

Yet you can catch yourself scripting in a beach scene. You are struggling perhaps to find a suitable location where the girl and boy first kiss. Without knowing it, you have set it on a beach on a hot, idle day. Or you can catch yourself scripting in an "ethnic touch", some ritual having to do with the shore. That is like playing to the gallery. You know it will touch one part of the audience who have never thought of the beach as anything more than sand.

I believe the escape from temptations of this kind is to write for your own people. It is a theme I will probably come back to again and again, because I do not think we have really learnt the lesson yet. I know that I have not. I suddenly catch myself playing to every audience, hardly aware that I am doing it.

For instance, during the development of the screenplay for *Ngati*, there was some well-meant pressure to provide a clue why Sally, the young Maori woman played by Connie Pewhairangi, returned from

the city to Kapua, the tiny village which was her birthplace. In terms of the general run of drama we have inherited by way of BBC television series and US telefeatures, there were plenty of plausible options. She might have had a relationship fly apart in the city; she might have contracted something; she might have wanted to explore an alternative lifestyle; she might have been pregnant. I am sure any television script department around the world could have come up with a dozen motives.

But young Maori return home for deep-seated reasons which, though felt instinctively by other Maori, are obscure to outsiders. There are many Maori phrases for it, like "going back to my bones", or "wanting to be with my whanaunga for a bit". They are reasons that are not much talked about. It is accepted that there are times when the bones call, when it is important and natural to go back to be, as Tuhoe people put it, "cleansed by the winds of Tawhirimatea". The community respects those who answer the call to return to their ancestral land. The fact that they have come back is physical evidence enough. Whether the returners are escaping from the cops or just want a bit of space is immaterial. The children of the land have returned to the land.

In the climate within which we script, it is so easy to "explain" why the young woman returned. Once you do that, you are writing for the general audience, for the majority culture, not for your own culture. In fact, the film is quite specific about why the young woman returns. She says in the pub in front of her friend Jenny, "Dad, with his job likely to go. Mum with another bloody kid on the way. And Ropata [her young brother] is not well at all, you know." She adds, in a quiet way one sometimes does to a special friend, "I'm scared for Ropata, Jenny. I haven't told anybody else that."

To a Maori audience, that is explicit, even too explicit. The sense that her family is in trouble has called her home. I do not think such callings are the special preserve of Maori people, but I am surprised that some Pakeha audiences hanker after some other motivation, something more "dramatic".

A touching moment for a Maori audience is when the woman has become fed-up with the usual family tensions and visits an old lady in the village. "I come home and all I can do is argue with them. Stupid of me, eh!"

The old woman reassures her. "You're a good kid. They both need you." Of course, the woman is paying tribute to one who has returned, but I do not think every audience senses that.

I am in the middle of sketching out a feature film script for what I hope will be my next film, *Te Rua*. It concerns a group of Maori men who set out to regain possession of their tribe's artistic treasures, currently held – so the story has it – in West Germany. A key character is Rewi, an urbane Maori who has spentmuch of his professional life in Europe. The strain on his family has become too much, and his wife Mere has taken the children back home. Despite being a sophisticated woman in her own right, Mere takes up labouring work in the shearing sheds, a job she trained for in her youth. Rewi comes back to New Zealand some months after his wife. He has pulled out of a major business deal and is treated as a king in the business circles of the capital, but on his return he learns that his wife has not only taken on a "low-class" job, but has also started living with Steven Ropata, a man who drives a truck for the local fisheries company. Once his business commitments are over, Rewi heads back into the country to look for his wife. He finds her working in a shearing shed. I have written the scene this way:

The international negotiator stands framed in the giant doorway opening out onto the loading ramp. Across the tightly-packed bales and the sorted piles of dags, he can see Mere, who is not taking the slightest bit of notice of him. The rest of the gang bend their backs to work.

Rewi pushes through the bales. The suede coat suits the image well – the mafia boss coming to collect what is owing to him. Rewi finds it humiliating to see her there, this wife of his, the woman he once took to some of the most refined restaurants in Europe, now a mere wool-classer. Mere, bright and breezy, with a rolled fleece in her arms, kisses Rewi lightly on the cheek.

MERE: "I've organised the old family home for you. Your sister's away tonight but she'll be back on the bus tomorrow afternoon. She asked if you would feed the pig."

Rewi stares at her, his eyes as black as those of a vindictive gangster who has forgotten how to fire his murder weapon. He jerks around to the rest of the shearers, some of whom are his own relatives. He maintains his height and his squared shoulders as he moves around the gang, shaking hands, as is the custom. He leaves the lead shearer, William Ropata, till last. He hongis him forcefully.

REWI: "You're William Ropata. Your grandfather on your mother's side was Hepi Ropata. Hepi Ropata's father was Rewi Whaanga. My name. Your second brother is called Steven Ropata. He shifts fish for Gisborne fisheries."

Rewi leaves the shed in what he considers a proud way.

When some Maori read this proposed scene, they laugh. "He used whakapapa to nail him." Whakapapa is lineage, genealogy, history. Rewi did not need to punch Steven Ropata's brother, William. He simply reminded him of their blood connections and, given the circumstances, that would be humiliating enough. He drove the knife deeper by reminding the offending family that a common ancestor carried his name, Rewi Whaanga. By mentioning whakapapa and a shared name in front of others, Rewi made his feelings clear to the others much more effectively than if he had resorted to some gross physical attack..

Perhaps you have similar traditions within your own culture, and no doubt other cultures have such traditions too. But from where I am sitting, I can imagine some debate coming up about this scene and others like it.

"OK. I accept that what Rewi does is culturally accurate, but how do you expect the rest of us to understand that? You will have to put in more explanation, give more background, or you are going to alienate your audience."

My only defence against that valid observation is rather a high-handed response:

"Well, I am not writing for you. I am writing for a Maori audience. They will understand what the scene means." And my homely kind of audience research among the Maori community – showing the script to a couple of trusted Maori mates – proves to me that Maori people will understand. My sample Maori audience chuckles at what Rewi

does. He manipulates the use of whakapapa in a way that is both unconventional and conventional. It is unconventional in that he uses it in public to put his wife and her new man in their places, and it is conventional in that the citing of whakapapa is often used to assert legitimate status.

Again I come back to my main point – who are we scripting for? There was a time when we made films to open a window on our own culture. No longer. If you are writing for your own people, explaining everything is something you can leave to others.

You might recall that little scene in *Ngati*, where the priggish Australian, sole passenger on the local bus, is coming along the coast road to the village of Kapua. The bus is held up by a mob of cattle. A Maori on horseback borrows some matches off the bus driver and then rides his horse along the length of the bus, looking to see who is travelling into town. He peers through the windows and spots the white passenger propped up in a pompous way. He hauls his horse around, stares with nose almost pressed to the glass of the window, and knocks on the window to attract the attention of the newcomer, who stares determinedly ahead. The newcomer is not going to admit the presence of a rude native. He then rides back to the front of the bus to ask the driver "Who is the flash fella in the back?"

Many Maori viewers laugh from the gut at this scene. It suggests exactly what many want to do – and what some of our more cheeky relations actually do – to "have a jack" at the Pakeha. Even though the shot flowed as one unit, I was advised by my producer, John O'Shea, to cut a chunk out of the middle. He felt that the newcomer would have turned to the man on the horse when he knocked on the window. I had directed the actor to stare fixedly ahead through the whole episode, but John argued that it would have been a most peculiar human who would not have acknowledged the rough horseman in some way. I happily accepted John's advice, and it so happened that we had a shot of the bus driver that could be dropped in without interrupting the flow of the scene. But I still wonder whether Maori audiences might have missed out on what could have been a gem for them.

It is one of the most political shots in the film. It shows the native

having the master in a situation where he cannot escape being peered at, just in the way the Labour, Justice and Education Departments, and so many other authorities have peered at Maori people for years. In staging the shot in the way I did, I was quite conscious that I was playing directly to an as yet unseen Maori audience, but during the edit I weakened and chose to play for both audiences.

A striking example for me of a Maori communicator being uncannily faithful to the culture and not bending to the demands of other communication traditions, comes in a few lines from Patricia Grace's novel, *Potiki.* Patricia is among the country's top writers and this, her second novel, is my favourite among the books I have read from authors who have a "third-world" background.

One of the key characters is a young woman called Tangimoana. She is in her early twenties and a born leader. The community has just suffered a setback. A flood – caused, as we are later to find out, by developers deliberately diverting the river – sweeps away the communal gardens on which the village depends for a livelihood. Relations come from all over the district to help clean up and replant. Patricia writes:

> During that time Pena fell in love with Tangimoana but she was not ready to be in love with anyone.
> ."I need him though," she said. "And that might almost be the same."
> Pena thought it was enough and they have been together much of the time since then.

And that's it! Four sentences.

Love is as important an ingredient in Maori life as in any other, but the thing is that it is talked about differently. To dwell at length on the progress of a relationship would seem indulgent or maudlin among Maori, and this shows up in many small ways. The "dinner-for-two" phenomenon does not exist among Maori, not only because very few Maori can afford a meal at a good restaurant under candlelight, but because most feel that to eat in isolation makes for a dreary meal. The best meal is when your cousin drops by out of the blue and you have to stick a bit extra in the pot. Couples happily fit their love-life around

such arrivals. The "honeymoon" phenomenon is not too widespread among Maori either. The honeymoon means the couple bolts the door for a week or two – your relations can't drop by, that aunty who loves to call on the telephone at 2 a.m. doesn't know where to get hold of you, and you wind up eating on your own in the evening.

I mention these phenomena because they are just two amongst a huge array of love settings that are much favoured in the cinema of the majority culture. We are familiar with such imagery, but the alien values under the imagery can creep into what might look to be, on the surface, Maori images. I doubt that any Maori writer would write a dinner-for-two scene into a film. A tender exchange between two people is much more likely to be set in a crowded communal dining room, squeezed in between laying dishes and passing a pot of tea along the table. But what are the words that are said? What is the body language? Are the pupils dilated? Is the breast heaving? It is so easy to script and direct such an exchange in a way that would fit just as easily into a traditional dinner-for-two setting, without even realising you are doing it.

I suspect that audiences, conditioned as they are by some decades of imagery from the majority culture, are rather greedy to have it both ways – to have the ethnic milieux but still demand the established conventions in dialogue and body language.

The following is a plausible scene in Maori life. A couple is at home in the evening making love in their room. The front door to the house is likely to be unlocked. Some friends drop around uninvited. They might have brought some food and a few bottles of beer. They sense the house is rather quiet. One puts the beers in the fridge and the other taps on the bedroom door to announce their arrival. The man calls out to say they will be out soon. One of the visitors lights up the stove and begins getting food ready, and a beer is shared. It is of no concern to the visitors how long it takes before the couple emerge. When the two come out, there are likely to be one or two wisecracks and then the evening settles down to the business of food and talk.

This type of scene happens over and over again in many communities around the world. Each community will have its own way of acting out the details, and precisely the way they do it will give the scene its own

ethnic or cultural flavour. I might say, in passing, I would find this scene difficult to direct, because it would be hard to steer through the prurient fixations that less earthy cultures seem to bring with them.

So we have a scene with an "ethnic" flavour and audiences are charmed to see something authentic which they can enjoy vicariously. But what happens in the bedroom? We have had such a barrage of bedroom images from the west over the years that it is difficult not to imitate them by shifting intimate dialogue from the marae dining room to the bedroom. It is difficult not to show the human body (and what shaped bodies have been cast?) in the way the French and British do. Unwittingly, you can create a "honeymoon" dialogue and honeymoon images right within a genuine ethnic context.

The wearying thing is that the audience, through the producer and the financiers, are pushing you for both images – the genuinely ethnic and the honeymoon exchange. If one or the other element is missing, your script might be judged to need further work. In this situation, I draw inspiration from lines like those few written by Patricia Grace about the relationship between Pena and Tangimoana. I cannot imagine Patricia countenancing a Swedish honeymoon scene between these two characters, not because she is a prude, but because she would insist that that way of portraying human contact is alien.

I worked among a group of young Maori people once and there was one woman with two children who had had an especially bad deal from men. Each child was from a different man, and each man was still hanging around. Both men had beaten her and there were times when she would be afraid they were going to show up late at night and be violent towards her or the children. The group was very protective of this woman, but hardly anything was said. "Was it okay last night? Did you have any hassles?" That was about all that was spoken. I am quite sure that if she was really having further trouble, some in the group would have been prepared to go around to her house, sleep the night on the couch, and pulverise anybody who tried to get through the door.

What ready material for the drama system of the majority culture. How easy to have the man turning up at 2 a.m., the rain beating on his shoulders, the children cringing in bed. Portraying the scene that

way would be to "Hollywood-ise" a fact of life for which Maori people have their own code. To take it to the extreme: a very outspoken political analyst here, Donna Awatere, wrote a major paper on what Maori sovereignty might mean. She spoke about the control of land, the legal rip-offs, and other things. She talked bluntly about how Maori men tended to prefer to team up with Pakeha women and how demeaning that was for the pride of Maori women.

She talked about rape too. As I understand it, her view is that rape, violent and all that it is, is not something that Maori women can afford to dwell on interminably. No Maori male ought to be sanguine about rape; it is all too prevalent in the Maori community. Donna's point, though, is that if Maori women become obsessed with the struggle against such violence, they will lose the energy to struggle on a broader front. The majority culture likes to portray the quirks of life. Rape can be the beginning of 90 minutes viewing. But what say you set out, as I perceive Donna did in her paper, by saying that rape is a trivial thing, merely a part of the general violence? Where does that leave a script assessor from the majority culture?

There are crass examples of how one might be persuaded into the patterns of thinking of the majority culture when it comes to working through a script project. A man from Hollywood, Robert McKee, came to New Zealand recently to lecture the industry on how to write successful drama scripts. Of *Ngati*, he said a problem was that there were three intertwined plots which did not link together. In my view, he missed the point. The linking was under the umbrella of the community. Life goes off in different directions in a community. The link is that it is all happening at the same time without pat linking devices.

Robert McKee's suggestion for knitting things better was to tie at least two of the streams together. One plot involves the closing of the local sheep slaughtering works, and another, the illness of the young boy. His suggestion was that the boy's illness could have been hooked to the slaughter works by way of a pollution problem; the slaughter works polluted the bay and the boy contracted his mysterious illness from swimming in the bay.

Daft as that idea seems to me, I have sat in on script discussions which have attempted to do exactly that sort of plot-stitching. Though

these lectures cost a tidy sum, the majority of the top people in the industry went, and for some months the town bubbled with confidence about how to do successful film scripts. I was lucky enough to be in India at the time.

I have been trying to stress how we are trying to think through what it means to address one's own people first. An example of how that might come unstuck occurred during the pre-production of the documentary *Te Urewera*.

We were up in the mountains and our research team was sounding out some of the old women to see what we might talk about when we returned to film. The conversation had just got under way when our team popped what I suspect is one of those questions westerners ache to ask people from so-called primitive cultures: "Did you have any plants for contraception?"

The women looked blank. After a time they said, "No, but we have many plants to make the babies come."

A book could be written on the special place children have in the Maori community, so I am not going to attempt to analyse it here. To those from the majority culture who might be tempted to look down on the desire of Maori couples to have many children, I can only say, tread carefully.

But here, I was making a film for the majority culture and the question was perfectly legitimate from their point of view. It is a question they will have on the tip of their tongues right through the programme and, if not answered, they might feel cheated.

We did not ask about plants for contraception. Nor did we do another tempting thing – to explore on film why Maori people have such confidence and pride in the birth process. That would have been to pander to an outsider's misplaced curiosity in another culture's customs. My perverse attitude is that if people want those sorts of questions answered, they should go to ask the community themselves.

With all the introspection about how we got where we are and thinking out how we should avoid what is foreign, we probably do not put enough energy into how we get on and do things right now in the

elusive "Maori way". But there are glimmerings. Tama Poata, the writer of *Ngati*, insisted that there should be no heroes in the film. In a Maori community everybody counts: the person who is getting a little too high and mighty is brought down a touch, and the one who is feeling small is raised up. He wanted to make a drama that respected those rules, making the community the hero, not this or that individual. I did my absolute best to direct the film in that spirit, not only because the writer wished it so, but also because it was something I had tried to make happen in other films. But at the time I did not fully appreciate what a drastic break with tradition was implied.

Western drama has come down to us from the Greeks. It makes a virtue out of focusing on individual trauma. A king is losing his crown, his wife, or his lands; a prince is wandering around wondering if he really is in this world. This long tradition of focusing on the individual has, at times, resulted in the absurd phenomenon whereby the writer asks us to sit for an hour or two watching just two people in a room trying to work out their sex life.

Of course we have inherited a rich tradition from the Greeks and others, and of course it is a joy to see a good production of a play like *Hamlet*. Yet in no way is tradition very mindful of the wider community. I know professionals have plenty of counter-arguments to this homespun thesis, but I flatly refuse to believe that western drama has ever been much inclined to make the community the hero.

Individualism is eschewed in the Maori world. Nothing is likely to isolate you faster than being in it for your own ends. In terms of the progress of a tribe, what does it matter if one marriage comes unstuck? No matter how savage the beating and no matter how glorious the romance, the tribe will move on. That, I think, is what Tama encapsulated in his script – a sense that the people continue, whatever the Hamlets or the Juliets of the world go through. The confidence to construct a drama with that outlook comes, in my view, from a knowledge of and a pride in the way the Maori community operates. Tama called it "telling it as it is".

I wrote a screenplay of Patricia Grace's *Potiki*. Patricia's style captures Maori ways of thinking beautifully, but much of the important thinking is told through prose descriptions rather than by dialogue. Early in

the book, Hemi, the cornerstone of the family on which the book is constructed, is made redundant. In his mind that is a blessing in disguise. He can return to work the communal land which has been idle since he was a boy. He walks quietly through the countryside back to his house where his wife and three children are waiting. This is a major moment in all their lives, and as he walks, Hemi is thinking about the past and the future.

Patricia writes of it in this style:

He would begin work on the almost completed fence. Next day he would sort out all the gear that was hanging in the shed. There were so many things in his head at that moment. It wasn't just the garden, it was everything, the whole place, the people. There was the sea. It was true they'd always used the sea and the shores, but they were not using them to the same extent as they had earlier. It was important now, important for their survival. There were all the things about the moon and the tides, wind and currents, and how to find the fishing grounds that needed to be told. Not just told, but shown. Then apart from the land and the sea, apart from the survival things, there were their songs and their stories. There was their language. There would be more opportunity now to make sure that they, the older ones, handed on what they knew.

The above is a set of snippets from a passage about Hemi that goes on for four pages. When I came to this scene, I ground to a halt which lasted for days. It was most important that the thoughts running through Hemi's mind were made accessible, but I did not want to do it through dialogue. I did not want these sentiments coming out in the kitchen late at night, with Hemi talking to his wife Roimata in the plain terms natural to a man from a farming background. I wanted to capture something of the nobility of Patricia's words – but how?

In the end I wrote the scene as follows. The dialogue is from prose taken from various lines tucked within Patricia's four pages.

Hemi eases his shoulders in the late sun. He walks to the fence and marks off their land. It has been in pasture for years. He strolls along the fence, noting the missing or broken battens, and checks whether the stay on the corner post is too rotten to save. Roimata follows him, her arms held easily across her chest.

Hemi walks onto the pasture block and Roimata still follows. The sky and the sea are purple. Hemi's boots brush through the unchecked grass. He makes circles with his arms as he looks across the block, first south, then north, as a farmer who has been forced to leave his soil fallow and now has a hundred plans. Roimata tags a little behind, breathing the new air and their unspoken ideas for the land. She catches sight of a lip of shell that has strayed from the beach and uses the pretext of wanting to prise it from the mat of grass as an excuse to squat as youngsters do.

HEMI: (to Roimata) "You were the pigtail girl. Waiting every morning holding the gate open at the school paddock when I brought my sister on the horse. You were so good to my sister. None of us forgot that. I can't imagine a life with anyone else."

Hemi paces through the grass, talking to the shore, the wind – to all the people. In the evening light, Roimata's physical beauty is very apparent. It is her quiet pride, however, that catches the eye. It is not the pride of a mawkish teenager, but the pride of a person listening to a speaker on the ground in front of a meeting house who is condensing all the thoughts of the people and presenting those thoughts on their behalf.

HEMI: "My grandfather taught me everything to do with planting, tending, gathering, storing and marketing. He taught me about the weather and the seasons, the moon phases and the rituals to do with growing. He said I was being given this knowledge on behalf of our people. It wasn't for me.
And there is the sea. There are all the things about the moon and the tides, winds and currents, and how to find the fishing grounds, that need to be told.
My other work, that was only a temporary thing. I've always known that. I've always known that one day I would return to the land and that the land would support us again."

And the scene continues.
The shape of this scene is drawn directly from whaikorero, or formal talk. This kind of oratory is used on both grand and humble occasions. The speaker will rise to his feet and deliver the talk to the whole assembled group. He is not to be interrupted. He will round out the talk with anecdote, reflections, reminders of the past, and humour.
There are many subtleties to whaikorero and I am in no way equipped to comment on them, except in a superficial way. I do know, though,

that it is a way of encapsulating thoughts orally (such speeches are never written) and presenting those thoughts publicly, to the whole people. It is an opportunity to present one's deepest feelings without embarrassment. Hemi's speech to Roimata is in that vein – the body language, the type of words used and the confidence behind the words. A Maori actor could play out that scene as whaikorero.

I shall have to leave it to the critics some time in the future to judge whether using the whaikorero model was appropriate in this case. For myself, I shall not forget the moment of elation when I suddenly saw that it might be possible to make use of the form. From that day the rest of the script flowed easily. I called on other cultural forms (especially a dance form called haka) to retain the spirit of Patricia's book.

The thought that comes to me from this is that we have opportunities to look into our own culture to evolve forms that might express our thinking in a more satisfactory way. It was actually a great relief and encouragement to have one's writer insisting on no heroes. It was exciting to work with the whaikorero and haka forms. We are only at the beginning of the road, but as the years go by, we might come to develop styles that are attractive and accessible to other cultures.

Of course, scripting touches all aspects of production. A culturally intact script could easily fall apart, culturally, in production. One scene in *Ngati* involved the two young women talking things through in a pub. Sally, played by Connie Pewhairangi, and Jenny, played by Judy McIntosh, were scripted to have equal weight in the scene, and I thought equal weight was important because it would help to demonstrate how in New Zealand, at some levels at least, Maori and Pakeha can get along just fine.

But in the first edit of the scene Jenny, the Pakeha, was favoured to the point where it became her scene. I think it was simply that Judy McIntosh was a more comfortable actor to present; her presence and diction were familiar. Connie's wasn't, at least not to a Pakeha audience. In fact, I cast Connie very deliberately. In Maori terms, Connie has the presence of the girl next door – the Maori girl next door. She almost vanished in favour of the Pakeha girl next door.

Casting can be a cultural issue too. *Ngati* has enjoyed some acclaim abroad as well as at home, but one of the awards I treasure most came

from an activist in Hawaii. "I want to thank you for putting our women on the screen." Leslie Kukoloio was saying how angry they were that for many years the industry had cast the classic stereotyped south sea islands beauties. I felt very proud that he chose to compliment our team on choosing young women familiar to us.

We have had some rather angry exchanges with our own writers, who feel frustrated that they do not have more power over the way their material is handled in production. This is, of course, a universal problem. It is rare to find a writer who is satisfied with the way his or her work emerges on the screen.

It is very simple for a writer to have complete control. Control only has to be specific when the rights are sold. Do you want to control the colour grading, the delivery of every line, which shots are cut into the edit? Fine. All that can be written into a contract. The only problem is that unless the writer has very solid experience in film-making it is hard to imagine any director, actor, art director, editor, director of photography or costume designer wanting to work on a production on that basis.

On the other hand, I sympathise with our writers' concerns. The technical machine has grown from a Pakeha base and Maori experience of using that machine for Maori purposes is new. A good script can fall apart in casting and over which actors are favoured in the edit. Every writer, from whatever culture, has fears of that kind, but at present those fears hang rather more heavily on Maori writers.

Until the screening on Television New Zealand of the five-part dramam series, *E Tipu, E Rea,* in November 1989, there had not been even five minutes of Maori drama on television in the whole 27 years of the network's existence. Not Maori drama as we define it – drama conceived, executed and presented by Maori. In October 1987 we decided, through Te Manu Aute, to challenge television on this matter. In recent years, television in New Zealand has been making up to 40 hours of local drama annually. We pushed for just three hours of Maori drama, even though, politically, it might have been possible to win three times that amount. We do not have trained Maori to handle more than the modest three hours, and so Pakeha people would come to dominate anything larger. There are established channels for getting

funding for drama, from television and from the New Zealand Film Commission, but we chose to bypass them. It then fell on our shoulders to come up with another mechanism. Phase I involved getting any funding at all. There were the usual arguments: "But we provide drama for the whole country. We have many Maori people in our dramas. Why should Maori drama be special anyway?" We won through that one by saying "Stop calling yourself New Zealand Television – call yourselves white New Zealand Television."

Besides, the major players were ready for a change. A package of good Maori drama could be a very marketable product, given the international status of Maori writers such as Keri Hulme, Witi Ihimaera, Patricia Grace, Hone Tuwhare and others. Once we had reached agreement on an allocation, we entered into Phase II. How should the funds be dished out? The natural thinking of the system was to channel funds down through the pipelines already in place on a step-by-step basis, as is normal for any production in this country. Development funding was made available, but the second payment would be contingent on satisfactory script and production packages being put forward.

We flatly refused to accept this system. It would have meant judges from the majority culture assessing what was appropriate. We said we were not going to approach our writers on Maori terms with that kind of judiciary lurking in the wings. Better to wait another 26 years.

Phase III was concerned with setting up a Maori trust under Maori control. Funding would be fed in large lumps to the trust by the investors, New Zealand Television and the New Zealand Film Commission, who would have no right to ask to what projects the money was being allocated. The trust would undertake to provide three hours of Maori drama and how it did it would be its own concern. And so the *E Tipu, E Rea* series came to be created. The arrangement under which it was achieved set an historic precedent in our country for both Maori and Pakeha film-makers.

It is claimed that the pen is a thing of power. I think that – when among strangers – it can be useful to have the power of production control behind that pen as well.

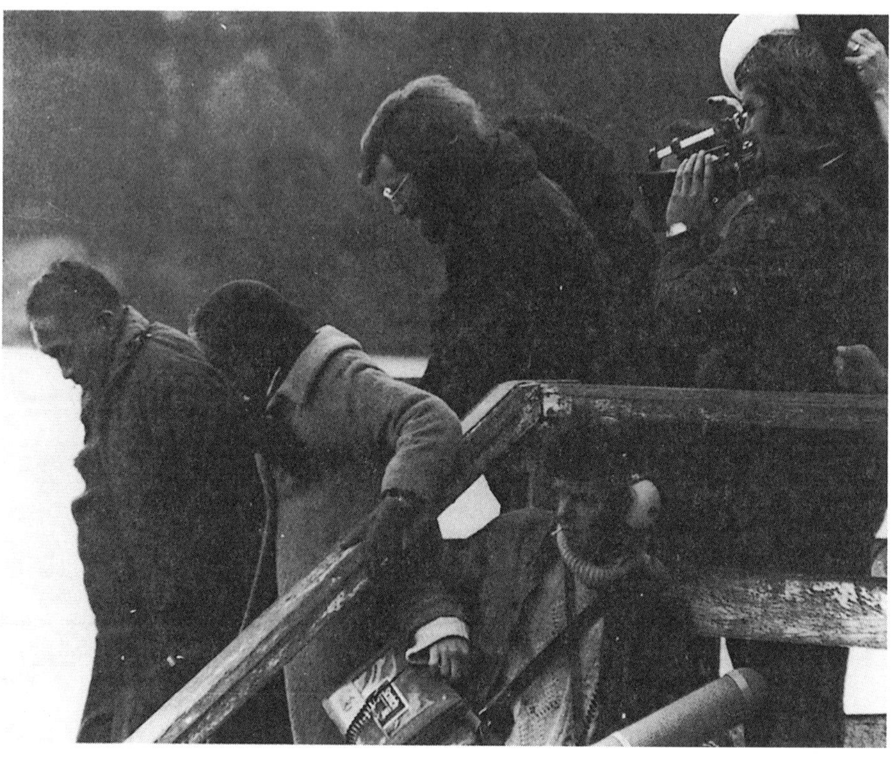

Cameraman Keith Hawke and soundman Craig McLeod film Te Uira Manihera and Herepo Rongo in 1972 for the first programme of the *Tangata Whenua* series, "The Spirits and the Times Will Teach". In the centre of the photograph is series writer/interviewer Michael King. Without Michael's skills and incredible commitment this landmark series would never have been made.

Pacific Films

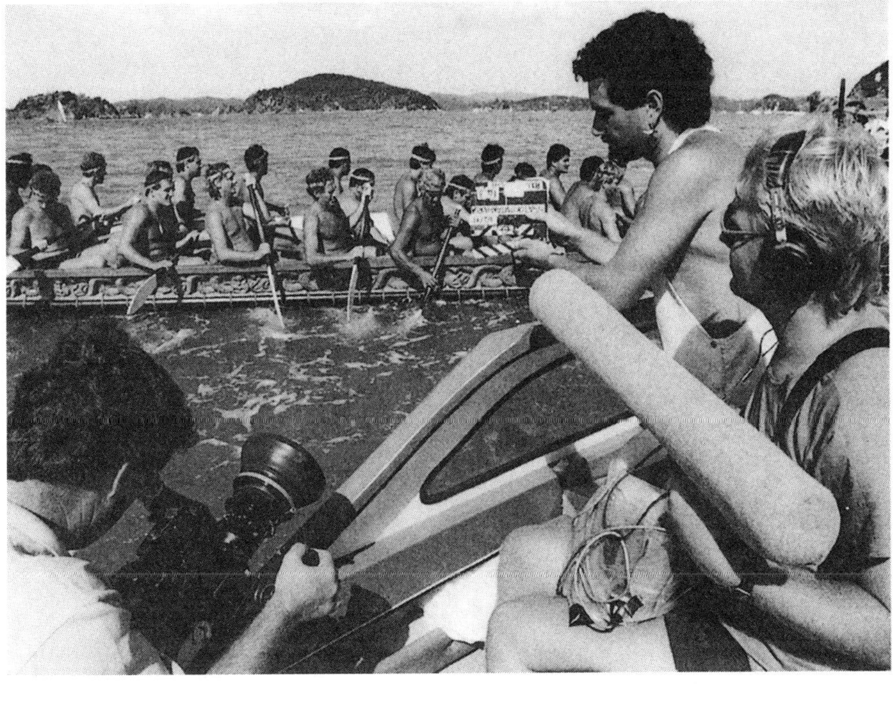

Director Tainui Stevens instructs his sound man and cameraman during the shooting of *Rere Ki Uta: Rere Ki Tai – The Voyage*. This independent 30-minute 16mm documentary shows the world's largest war canoe crossing open ocean in a 10 hour non-stop journey, and, as the producer's publicity puts it, "As it was for their ancestors, the trip is [for the 100 paddlers] a voyage of discovery and fulfilment – an awakening of being Maori."

Tai Tokerau Productions

OPPOSITE: On location in July 1989 for *Thunderbox*, one of the five 30-minute programmes of the Maori drama series *E Tipu E Rea*. At top, actor Wi Kuki Kaa (left) and writer Bruce Stewart. Below from left, camera operator Rewa Harre, director Lee Tamahori and camera assistant Fred Renata.

Te Manuka Film Trust, John Miller

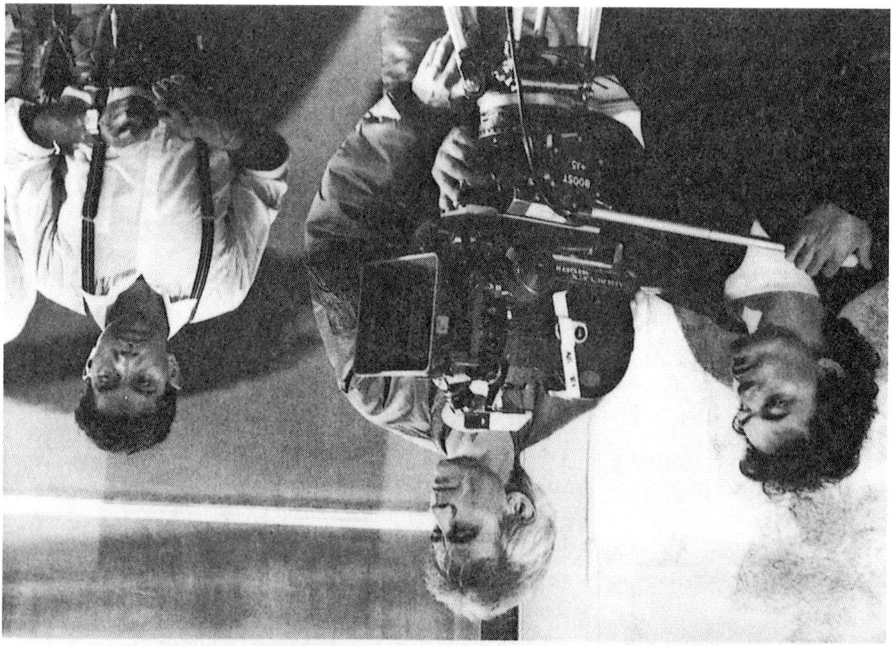

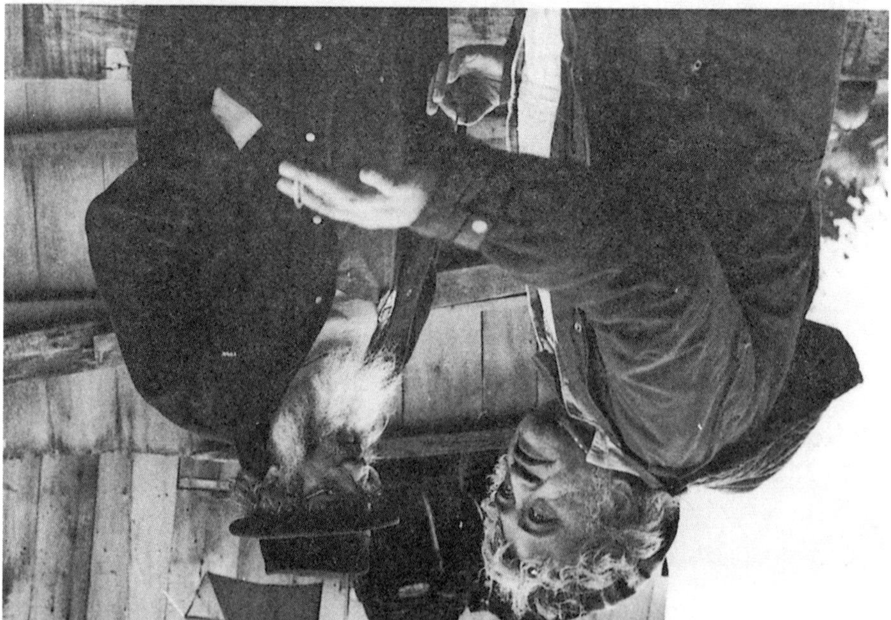

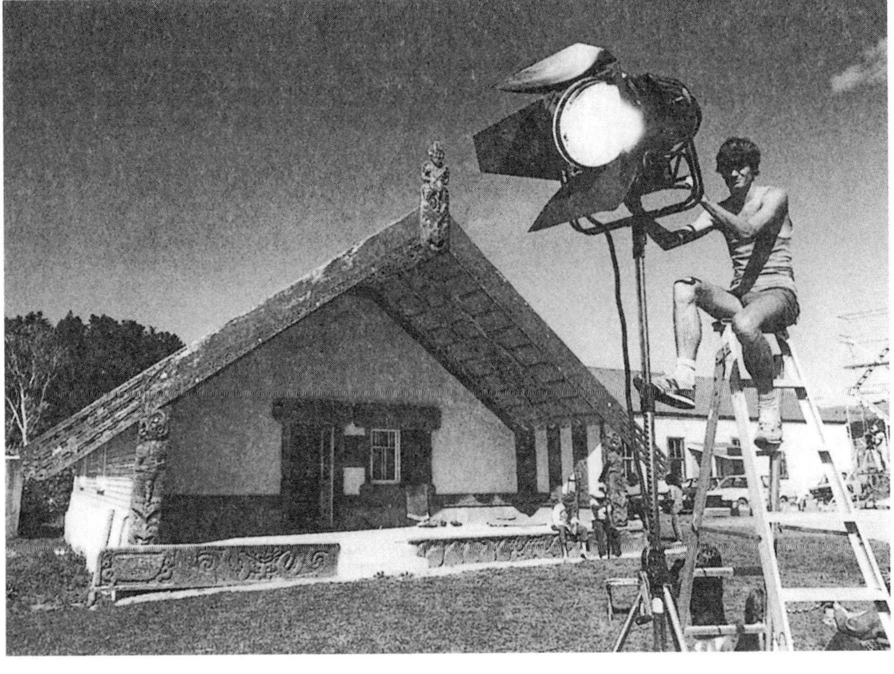

Generator operator Kevin Riles sets a HMI light in front of Iritekura meeting house in Waipiro Bay during the filming of *Ngati*. This marae became a base during the production. Many of the crew slept in the meeting house and, for five weeks, the local people took charge of cooking three meals a day for up to sixty people at a time.

Pacific Films, John Miller

5

The Script Abroad

No matter how strongly motivated you are to pick your script up off the typewriter and bring it to life in the field in ways that you know, even dimly, are somewhat closer to your own culture, you soon learn that some established industry practices can trip you up on location. Often it comes down to seemingly trivial things.

In the Maori world, children are ever present. No matter where you go you have kids under your feet and, like it or not, you look after them. Nothing is likely to poison the atmosphere more quickly than somebody being harsh on the children.

When filming in any community, people, especially the kids, are curious to see a little of how "Hollywood" works. They poke their noses round the door, giggle a bit, and are dead keen to see how it is done. It is standard practice to clear the set when the time comes to shoot. "Clear the set." When the kids start poking their noses around the door, you can either kick them out – "CLEAR THE SET!" – or invite them in, telling them to sit down, shut up, and have a good look. After ten minutes they are bored and go off to play real games.

In the early days of shooting *Ngati*, some of the crew were puzzled by my insistence that the kids be allowed to "have a jack", as we call it. The crew had legitimate concerns. Safety, for one thing; there is a lot of high-voltage electricity running round a film set. But I am proud to say that "clear the set" was not used once during the shooting of *Ngati.* Had we enforced that industry practice, as far as the local people were concerned, our names would have been mud.

Then there is the matter of "time" – "Maori time", as it used to be called contemptuously in New Zealand, and I notice that "Hawaiian time" is used by some Pakeha in Hawaii. No doubt there is a similar racist phrase used against your own culture. Some funny things happen when you try to get a crew comfortable with Maori time.

One morning during the shoot of *Ngati* we had a scene involving a dozen or so of the old women. The lighting crew (a very good one) had rushed down their breakfasts and had the lights rigged well within the allocated time. They were proud of their efficiency and wanted to get on with the scene, but the old women were nowhere to be seen. I asked one of the production team, a Maori woman, what the old women were up to. She said that the women were costumed and made up, but while they were waiting for the technical crew to complete the rig they had started a game of cards and were in the middle of a hand. She didn't think it was a good idea to call them out until the hand was finished, and I agreed.

The production woman went back to the old women to wait for a suitable lull in the game when she could break in. We figured on about a 10-20 minute delay. It was not a comfortable position for me, having revved up the crew to get the set lit early. "Why can't the production team deliver the talent on time?" they asked. I did not feel confident I could tell them. I thought that if they knew the talent was playing cards, there would be angry words.

After quarter of an hour, the crew was walking up and down behind me muttering that the lights were set and the camera was ready. There would be a pause and then they would repeat, "The lights are set." I turned to the crew and said, "Great. The lights are set. The camera is set. Why don't you make a movie?" I regretted taking the mickey out of a crew in that way, because their frustrations were genuine and – for those who have not had much experience of why Maori time is Maori time – excusable. But it does become draining when incidents of this kind occur regularly.

I did not have a first assistant director on the crew because I believed that for the *Ngati* shoot it was vital to respect Maori time – meaning "respect the way the community operates". That decision was controversial both before and during the shoot. It still gives me heartache, and still leaves some of the technical crew convinced that the production was badly organised. I would dearly love to have had a trained Maori first assistant, but there were none available at the time. There were some very sympathetic Pakeha first assistants, but I was worried that, in a crisis, their lack of appreciation of Maori time would have led

them to operate on Pakeha time and, as a consequence, we would have antagonised the community.

To compensate for the lack of a first assistant, we had a team of young Maori, new to the game. In terms of industry-type organisational skills the team fell down many times, sometimes gravely, but in terms of keeping the community bond alive the team did not falter once, or if it did, the damage was immediately repaired in typically Maori ways. The community was dealing with "cousies" after all. However, the lack of a first assistant director, in the mould to which the industry is accustomed, made for some insecurity among the crew. They felt the organisational side was a shambles, and that we were not going to get the production through on the tight schedule available to us.

The irony is that *Ngati* was shot in just five weeks. Few other New Zealand feature films operating on Pakeha time have been shot in anything like as short a period. And I still do not know of a first assistant in whom I could be utterly confident while handling the case of the old women playing cards (and many other incidents like it) in a Maori way.

There was another important piece in the production jigsaw puzzle. I decided not to use a dolly. There was a bit of flak over that both before and during the shoot. It was hinted that I was scared to use tracks; that I was secretly trying to make a documentary, and that I did not understand what is required for the big screen. But the reason for not using a dolly was simple. Given the cramped and scattered locations, and given new actors with no experience of hitting marks, we would have needed another two weeks to shoot the film. To compensate for not having tracks, we used the long lens (while panning with an actor) to help create a heightened sense of movement. It is over to the critics to say whether it worked or not.

We did have what I consider to be a failure on *Ngati*, one that I did not expect to arise. It had to do with creating a visual tapestry reflecting the physical details of Maori communal life. Day and night, there are always people about in the Maori community. In the middle of an important conversation an aunty might come in carrying a toddler who needs to be put to bed; somebody in the background might be wiping off the kitchen table, preparing for a couple of men who have

just returned from gathering seafood; a young girl might have dropped by to raid her friend's collection of t-shirts before taking off for a game of netball. This is the normal tapestry of life – but how to capture it on the screen?

Let's take an imaginary scene – a discussion among the elders in the meeting house. During such a discussion, the kids might be sneaking out to kick a football around, and a two-year old might have just awoken on the mattress and be in need of attention. If you were shooting a documentary, you would simply leave the lights up for an hour and quietly "ping off" the details. We weren't able to achieve this when shooting *Ngati.*

Rory O'Shea, as well as being a top-shelf feature film director of photography, is a superb documentary cameraman, and we have worked on many documentaries together. As a model of the kind of texture I was looking for in *Ngati,* I talked through a documentary sequence we had shot together in Nicaragua.

A family in a poor suburb of Matagalpa was holding a communal meal to commemorate the anniversary of the death of their son who, at the age of 18, had been exterminated by Somoza's agents. There were some 50 people gathered in the small courtyard – the young and the old, the influential and the overlooked. We did not have much time because when we arrived the event was nearing its close. Rory filmed like one possessed. He captured many special details – the faces of the family still sorrowing eight years after their son's murder; an old man lost in his own thoughts; the kids licking their plates clean; the parrot being fed on its perch on the yellow plastered wall. Many of the images were of such quality they would, in my view, grace any feature film, even though Rory was forced to shoot at speed using only available light.

I had hopes that we would be able to gather such additional imagery in certain scenes for *Ngati* – imagery I knew we would not have a hope of setting up formally. It was not to be. One difficulty was that we found it very difficult to turn from shooting the key feature film master shots (with all the pressure on the camera team that this involves) to shooting documentary detail, and having been a cameraman of sorts at one time myself, I know exactly what the crew felt.

I have only myself to blame for whatever disappointment I have in not gaining those little extra details. I should have taken more time to explain to the whole technical crew exactly why I believed those additional shots would be important in trying to enhance the community feel of the visual. But there were other pressures operating too. *Ngati* was a period drama and the costume department were naturally very proprietorial about just how each person was dressed. Fair enough, but it did make it a little tough to get shots of kids acting spontaneously while pottering around the meeting house if the costume crew were waiting to tuck in (or pull out) the kid's shirt before the camera was free to roll. Or if makeup were watching to add a touch of powder or to wipe away the drops of perspiration, and sound was waiting too, hoping for the snyc tracks of the kid's footsteps, the sniffles, a cough that might come. None of that is calculated to achieve the recording of intimate and unscripted detail.

Some suggestions were made as to how to set the production machine up so that it was flexible enough to gather the additional images – a second camera for instance. On *Ngati*, I doubt that a second unit would have worked, because the film was made up of a host of small scenes and the technical crew (lighting, grips, costumes, makeup) were necessarily geared to a narrow focus. Having a second unit would have meant the main crew would have had to think broadly, in tapestry fashion, and I doubt that we were capable of that, whether because of our previous experience in the industry here, or because of a lack of clear brief from me. Besides, we did not have the funds to operate a second crew.

My producer, John O'Shea, best put a finger on what I was about when he suggested that Rory, technically the boss of the first unit, should shoot on second camera. While that probably would not have been possible for financial reasons, it was a valuable comment for me, because it suggested that at least our team could appreciate the value of "secondary images" in creating a communal tapestry effect, even though at the time we were not to succeed in finding ways to gather them.

On larger films, *The Killing Fields*, for instance, street and village texture was created very skilfully by the use of massive staging. It is

unlikely we shall ever have the kind of budget necessary to pull off that same look off successfully. Besides, I am not convinced that this type of staging, despite its sophistication, comes very close to serving our needs, namely the need to bring forward the intimate detail that is part and parcel of community living as we know it.

Perhaps the reason we failed to move the system when we tried to get a better range of secondary images by using documentary techniques had (apart from my own inadequacies) to do with attitudes within the majority culture – a fear of mixing documentary and drama, and a compulsion to "get on with the story".

There is a mighty rupture between the documentary and drama traditions in the western film tradition. Of course, drama and documentary are different, and of course some degree of separation is healthy. But I can't help feeling the distance is too exaggerated at times. It is frustrating to be making a film which you know will be of great consequence to Maori people, but find yourself unable to use readily available techniques to gather images that you know will be treasured by them. You come to wonder whether you are being blocked by a production system that seems to separate drama from document-ary too rigidly. Just what is the relative importance of a beautifully delivered line from a lead actor and an image of a child being covered by its mother in a meeting house? My guess is that your answer depends on what culture you have been brought up in.

Some of the difficulties on location arise from a basic unfamiliarity with the culture. When there is a death, the body is brought to the marae and the immediate family and the old people remain with the deceased for something like three days, welcoming the mourners and acting as guardians of the protocol and rituals. The younger ones are charged with the task of feeding the visitors, which might well involve cooking for 500 people, and at major tangi (funeral), as many as 5000. The community usually has only a very few hours before having to provide food for those who have come to share the grief of the family.

On a marae the cooks are treasured. There is a strong rule that when the cooks call you to eat, you go and eat. There are good reasons for this. To feed, say, 100 people, then to clear the tables and feed another 100 people, takes hard work and the co-operation of many. A

dining room on a marae is not like a McDonald's or a high-class restaurant, where one expects to eat at will. Maori are trained to respect the call of the cooks. "Haere mai ki te kai." You do not have another cigarette, nor do you sit in the sun finishing a conversation. You move immediately.

Not so some Pakeha crew. Although their dilatory behaviour comes not from ill-will, but from a lack of appreciation of how things operate on a marae, it is not much fun having to go round asking your crew, one by one, to go in to lunch. On the surface, this kind of things is a trivial matter, but it has been such trivial matters that have created a strong move to train Maori crews.

The role of the cooks and the lack of understanding of their role on the marae created a vivid picture for me on *Ngati* of just how different cultures create and share images. There is a death in *Ngati*. In creating for film an impression of the customary tangi rituals, we had to respect certain rules. The graveyard was specially built because real burial grounds are sacred. No grave was dug – to dig a hole is to invite death. The coffin was kept out of sight until the last moment for the same reason. In many dramas involving a burial, the camera pushes in on the faces of the sorrowing people, and even goes down into the grave and looks up at the mourners for an effective dramatic angle. Such indelicacy is offensive to many Maori.

There are restrictions about food too. Food is never taken into the meeting house or on to a burial ground, and is certainly not taken anywhere near where the deceased is lying at a tangi. Nevertheless, the preparation and serving of food to visitors is an integral part of the tangi ritual. Within an hour of a person's death, responsibilities fall immediately on the shoulders of the younger people. Kumara (sweet potato), cabbage and seafood have to be gathered; mutton has to be killed; firewood has to be spilt.

How to blend that dimension into the narrative? During the preparation of the screenplay, there were some reservations about the propriety of including food so close to death. These were overcome easily enough, due to the determination of the writer, Tama Poata, a Maori from the area, who pointed out that food preparation was, and is, part of the normal procedure when death occurs. Our producer,

John O'Shea, accepted this, because he trusted Tama and me to know the basics of the culture.

On a feature film, the art department prepares the props for each sequence. Once shooting begins, the props are handed over to "standby props", whose responsibility it is to see that the props are placed on the set as the director wishes. The art department happened to be Pakeha, and the standby props person a Maori, Phil Taratoa. The night before we were due to shoot the men of the village cutting up the meat which would feed the mourners, Phil came up to me. It was 7.30 in the evening. Phil looked to me as if he might have been close to tears. He showed me what the art department had given him as props. He held in his hands two rolls of cooked roast beef, wrapped in clear plastic which they had bought at the supermarket. The two rolls would not have been enough to feed more than half a dozen men.

We made a hurried plan. Edward Kauraria, who managed a farm nearby, and Kingi Karataina, one of our crew, said they would get up at first light and kill two animals for our scene. That was not much fun for them, but being Maori, they understood the problem. Next morning, thanks to Edward and Kingi, we had two freshly-killed mutton carcasses available for the scene. I have since learned that to go behind the art department's back in this way is not the proper thing for a director to do, but they were being unhelpful by insisting that the two rolls of beef would be perfectly adequate.

I also felt I had a problem with the camera crew. After a conventional wide shot and a couple of the usual close-ups, they appeared to think they had got the scene and wanted to move on. I insisted we needed a series of close-ups of the men, and close-ups of what their hands were doing. I felt – rightly or wrongly – that the crew did not have their heart in these shots, thinking that the director had a fetish about food. We did get the shots, but hardly with enthusiasm.

When we came to edit this scene, our editing team seemed to feel that it was not in good taste, and would probably disappear from the edit at a later stage, so a wide shot was cut in the interim and it was left at that. It took some persuasion to convince our team to give that small scene the same loving attention given to other scenes in the film.

We had a flash-point argument right near the end of the edit. I was told "Don't tell us what funerals are about. We have been to funerals too, you know." Of course. Death is death and grief is grief. But the Maori way of encompassing death, the practical rituals, are different. If a relation of yours dies, Maori start cooking. If a Pakeha person dies, the body is left in a funeral parlour and the family telephones a caterer to make up club sandwiches. But in due course, we cut the scene to flow as I had hoped and it has remained in the film.

I repeat these in-house discussions with the greatest of affection for all the people involved. We had a good art department, a good editing team, and a good camera crew. I recount the experiences simply to highlight the point that sometimes it is not easy to hang on to the most basic of cultural values even when one has the authority.

The final irony is that the scenes of the men cutting meat may have to be removed from any versions offered for European television sales, apparently because Europe has strict rules about what is proper to show to family audiences.

I have lived for long spells in Europe. I noticed people buying red meat wrapped in clear plastic from the chiller in the supermarket, with little thought of who cut the throat of what they were eating. I have eaten in Europe, at times just 50 kilometres from major nuclear missile bases. As a native, one struggles to understand the enlightened ways of the civilised.

6

Talking In

For many years we have had a wonderful programme on New Zealand television called *Country Calendar*. Drama series, hard-nosed current affairs slots and smart new game shows have come and gone, but *Country Calendar* remains, and has become almost an institution.

As the name suggests, the programme shows rural life in our country – a family trying to make a go of it on steep, erosion-prone country; a young entrepreneurial couple experimenting with a new crop for the Japanese market; or a country sports day. The programmes are designed to be understood and enjoyed by all New Zealanders, 95 per cent of whom are urban dwellers who may not have mustered sheep or milked a cow in their lives. The material is presented in a way that does not demean rural life – the programme is as popular among farmers as "townies" – yet is attractive to those outside the farming community. You might say the programme makers are "talking out" from the farm to a world beyond.

In contrast, Radio New Zealand has a daily radio news bulletin for farmers called *Rural Report*. In this programme, farmers are talking to other farmers in their own language about their own concerns. To an outsider, the language is much more technical than that usually heard on *Country Calender* – stock units, pasture mixes, fertiliser regimes, spore counts, weight gains, dosing levels, and the like. The issues discussed also tend to be grittier – the likely impact on top-grade apple production following a sudden shift in the exchange rate of the New Zealand dollar against the German mark; the removal of a transport subsidy and its effect on the peach industry in the central South Island; or whether or not some new testing procedure suddenly imposed on beef exporters to the United States market is nothing more than a ruse to protect American producers from imported product

. . . and so on. Here we have farmers talking to farmers – people "talking in" as it were.

I enjoy both the "talk out" and the "talk in" approaches. Each has its place, but in the end, I find a "talk in" programme much more rewarding, even though I might not be able to catch all the nuances of what is being said. With *Rural Report* I feel as if I have been suddenly dropped in among farmers and am catching something of their real lives. It is the difference between being escorted through a paddy field in Sri Lanka by a local agricultural development officer, who tells you what crops are being planted there, what tonnages are expected this season, and so on, and sitting in the mud hut of a smallholder talking about water rates, freight subsidies, and how the dropping of trade tariffs has meant a flood of cheap chillis from southern India, which has distorted the local market so much that he is going to give up growing chillis completely and go on to God knows what. One is a tourist trip; the other, farmers' talk among farmers.

The film-maker working within the majority culture is caught slap bang between *Country Calendar* and *Rural Report* – between "talking out" and "talking in". On the one hand, there is – in the words of the Te Manu Aute constitution – a right and a responsibility for any culture to present itself to its own people in its own way – to "talk in". On the other hand, there is an awesome communications structure already established by the majority culture, which either shrieks ratings and returns, or seductively pleads to find out more about Maori culture. Whether the tones are honeyed or shrill makes little difference – it's "talk out" brother, or the scrap-heap for you.

My first work in the Maori community, the *Tangata Whenua* series, did involve talking out to the majority culture. The series explored questions that New Zealanders at that time wanted asked, questions like "What is the Maori attitude towards children?" We were so eager to put across to the majority culture what Maori values were all about that we set out to structure the series around headline captions such as: "Maori attitudes to land", Maori attitudes to death", and the like. Thank goodness the Maori community quashed that approach. Maori people simply do not think in such categories and no amount of media sleight-of-hand will inveigle them into doing so. In due course we came

to structure the series around a collection of community cameos.

There is no question that the *Tangata Whenua* programmes set out to convey to others something of what Maori life is like. The cameo approach disguised that purpose considerably and there was a political sub-text which gave the material a vitality not usually found in academic documents. Still, the series "talked out" in a way that I believe many Maori are now rejecting. The "talk out" approach has been tried, not only in film-making, but in many other areas too – in education, public broadcasting and publishing. By and large, the approach has failed. The majority culture seems to have ears like a sponge: you can talk your tongue off, year after year; the ears flap, but in the end you feel you have spent your life speaking to a great sponge which does not seem to learn, but which is ever eager to absorb more.

I have come to believe we need to be talking to our own people first – to be "talking in". Some Maori colleagues will disagree, perhaps, while others will have come to that position long before I have. And to our supporters in the majority culture, a policy of "talking in" might seem a proposal to close off Maori culture to anybody who is not Maori. Surely if a culture is healthy and optimistic, it can afford to be outgoing, giving freely to everybody? Trying to cope with this major objection has led me to wonder whether it might be helpful for us to think of our work as a different sort of marae – an invisible one, looking inward but open to all.

A typical marae has three buildings – a meeting house, where important talk is conducted and where people sleep; the dining room, where people cook and eat; and the ablution block. Marae are a combination of town hall, church, restaurant, sleeping quarters and playground. There are many rules of conduct on a marae, and while the rules differ a little from place to place, the broad rules are common to all marae across the country. You don't, for instance, take food into the meeting house. The guardians of any active marae will make sure the basic rules are adhered to. If you are not capable of accepting those rules, the local people will not be sorry to see you go, because in order to retain that special quality that makes a marae a marae, the guardians must insist that the marae complex is, before everything else, Maori. The slightest compromise on this principle reduces the

set of marae buildings and the land around them to nothing more than a motel-cum-conference centre – and that you can find in any part of the world.

The experience of spending a few days on a marae is special – the sense of communal living, the way talk is shared – and people usually find it uplifting. Quite a number of Pakeha conferences are now staged on marae so that participants have a brief opportunity to soak up another atmosphere and set of attitudes. At the same time, there are people who freak out at the very thought of going onto a marae. Some are simply shy because they are worried that they might not know what to do, but there are others who take a very arrogant attitude to what goes on on marae and wouldn't be seen near one for all the tea in China.

Perhaps if we were to look at our communications "word" as another sort of marae, we might say – in the style of the guardians of any marae – "You're welcome to come in, but please don't ask us to change the rules of the marae. If you help us keep our little marae painted and in good working order, we will have something that we as New Zealanders can all be proud of, be we white or brown. We will have something we can share with others, no matter what part of the world they come from. But if we change the rules, we will have a motel. We will have nothing to share with anybody."

As I see it, the way to keep the spirit of the young communications marae strong is to be absolutely rigid about operating it along marae lines. "When you enter this space, you will hear our people talking in their own way to their own people." I hope the examples I have given earlier, such as rejecting honeymoon imagery and not pressing the old women about what plants were used for contraception, give an indication of what I think is involved in keeping the communications marae strong. Proceeding this way is going to alienate some, but in the long run it seems better to keep the marae fires burning, waiting for the time when people will overcome their shyness or their hostility, than to turn the communications marae into a Hollywood motel.

In the instance of the plants for contraception, there are ways to answer the hidden questions that might be nagging in the heads of visitors to the marae. You could slip in cut-away shots showing plenty

of kids about, all of whom are treated with affection, or you could leave a couple of lines of conversation which hint at Maori attitudes towards children. I do not see this as changing the basis of the programme, but rather as a way of making the total outsider more comfortable.

I do not think this is turning inward in an unhealthy way. Rather, I see it as asserting a cultural confidence so that, if we shape things our own way, we shall come to make images that will be attractive to those humans on the planet who wish to enjoy them. I am not talking about minority programmes directed at a minority. I am talking about a minority being confident enough to talk with its own voice about whatever it chooses and as it does so, having a feeling that the talk will be of interest to others who wish to drop in.

To put it another way: I am not much interested in seeing a film made by Welsh people who want to explain their situation to the British authorities in London. The Welsh will have to make films of that kind from time to time, but I do not think I would go out of my way to view them. On the other hand, I would be very interested in watching a film made by Welsh communicators trying to make a metaphor for their own people, a film they would have made whether other people in the United Kingdom saw it or not. Some will say that economics insist a film must be made for the widest possible audience – for Americans, Dutch, Canadians, and perhaps Brazilians too. My view is that if a film has cultural integrity, it will have much more appeal to other cultures than if it were tailored for them.

A marae has another quality that tempers what, at first glance, might seem to be exclusiveness. The whole conduct on a marae is aimed at making people from other areas welcome and comfortable. No matter how steeped in tradition a marae is, and no matter how piously the local people invoke those traditions, if visitors feel they have not been brought in warmly and treated well, then the marae will be considered hollow and will die. When creating a communications marae, I think we must be conscious of that duty to offer suitable hospitality. You must not insult your guests, or let them feel they are being left on the outer. If we do not respect that most basic of marae rules, the communications marae we have striven so hard to set up

will be rejected, not only by the majority culture, but by our own people – and indeed, by them first.

I have seen it happen. A good Maori programme included one Pakeha who was interviewed a little aggressively. It was done in a much less aggressive way than he might have expected on many a Pakeha programme, but the tone of the interview felt out of place in a programme that was generally very Maori in spirit. That one aggressive note soured the programme for one or two of the older people, and they let that be known to the director.

Perhaps re-orienting communications towards a marae climate has as much to do with tone as direction. Maori conduct their affairs on a marae in a special way. The strident voice is not liked. Some fearfully strong points are made on marae, and sometimes these points are directed at an individual, but whereas such points in other meeting structures might cause people to walk out in anger or tears, they are made on the marae in such a way that people are kept within the fold. It would be unpardonable to humiliate somebody to such a degree that he or she would not set foot on the marae again – the old people would not stand for it.

Such a spirit can infuse film-making too. I am very conscious not to treat anybody in a way that would not be sanctioned on a marae. All film-makers have some code about treating people properly, of course, but a Maori film-maker has the marae tradition to draw on, a tradition that makes use of humour and anecdote more freely than other New Zealanders do in situations which are potentially confrontational.

What would happen in the unlikely event we got funding to make a programme on our people, to be specifically directed towards another indigenous culture such as yours? Should we "talk out" or "talk in"? I don't think there are many Maori communicators these days who would accept a commission to make a film designed to "talk out" to European cultures, but a project designed for you would be a special case. I suspect we should still "talk in". I think a well-crafted film on one of our land struggles, which we have made for our own purposes, would be of more interest to you than a film which set out to explain to you indigenous life as we know it.

So, in preacher fashion, I say that we should be talking to our own

people first, and that talk should be conducted in the spirit of the marae, a spirit that can generate a climate which is welcoming to all, precisely because it has been created from a confidence in being Maori and in conducting oneself as one does on a marae. And it at this point that umpteen Maori communicators will push the preacher right out of the pulpit because they have been doing what I am preaching anyway – particularly the younger ones. It would not cross their minds to act in any other way.

Still, we have to be realistic enough to recognise that this approach will never gain the ear of everybody, because there will always be some who only like going into those houses with which they are familiar. On the other hand, I feel that if – and only if – we build a house on Maori lines, we shall have a place into which we can invite people from any part of the world, a place that will be special for those who wish to enter. Such high and mighty sentiments come down to some pretty blunt matters.

When we were working to set up the Maori drama series, *E Tipu, E Rea*, a hui was called to explain the proposal, and as part of the weekend's talk, the organisers invited two people to speak who had had a great deal of experience in writing for television. The subject of their talks was "Writing for Television". In good faith, they launched off explaining how television needed scenes of a certain length, a number of sub-plots, and the like, explaining that you only have a certain amount of time to grab a television audience and that this was how television went about it. I sat there thinking, "But we are not writing for television, we are writing for screening on television."There is a big difference. How we "grab" our audience and which audience we are seeking is our own affair, because first we are talking to our own people. I must admit, however, that despite waving my finger in the air as best I could, I am not convinced that anybody grasped my point.

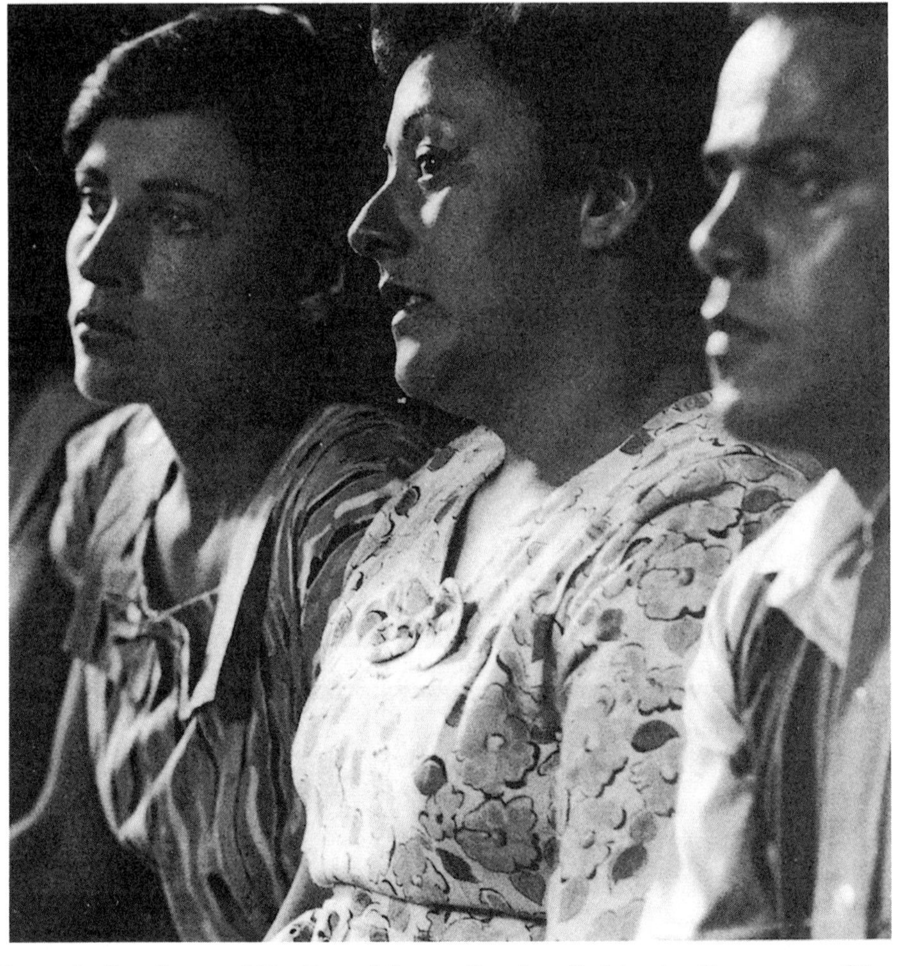

Towards the climax of *Ngati* a public meeting is called to give the owners of the major employer in the tiny village of Kapua – the meat-processing works – a chance to explain why the works is to be closed. Two of the lead characters, Jenny (left) and Sally discuss making a stand. Jenny is played by Judy McIntosh and Sally by Connie Pewhairangi.

Pacific Films, John Miller

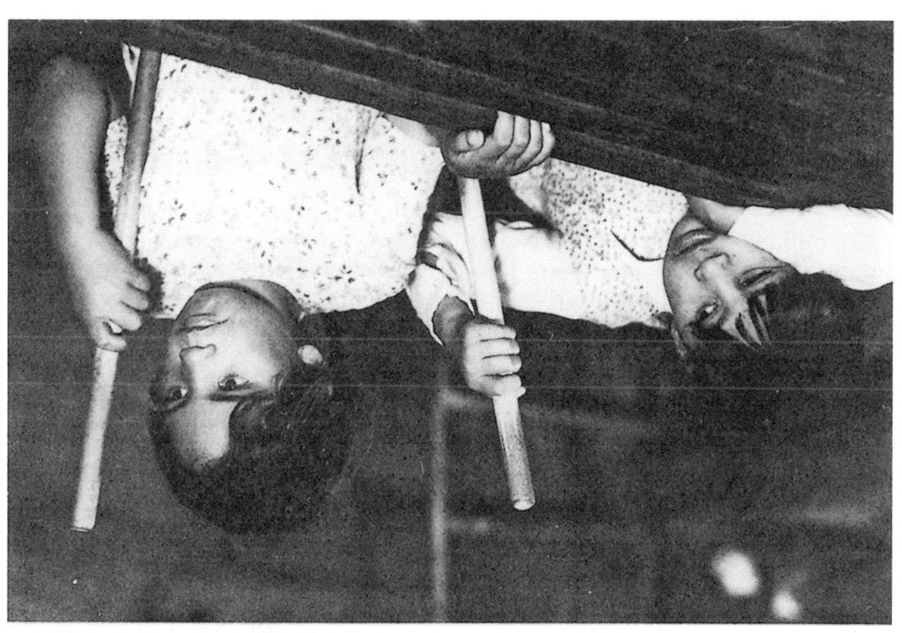

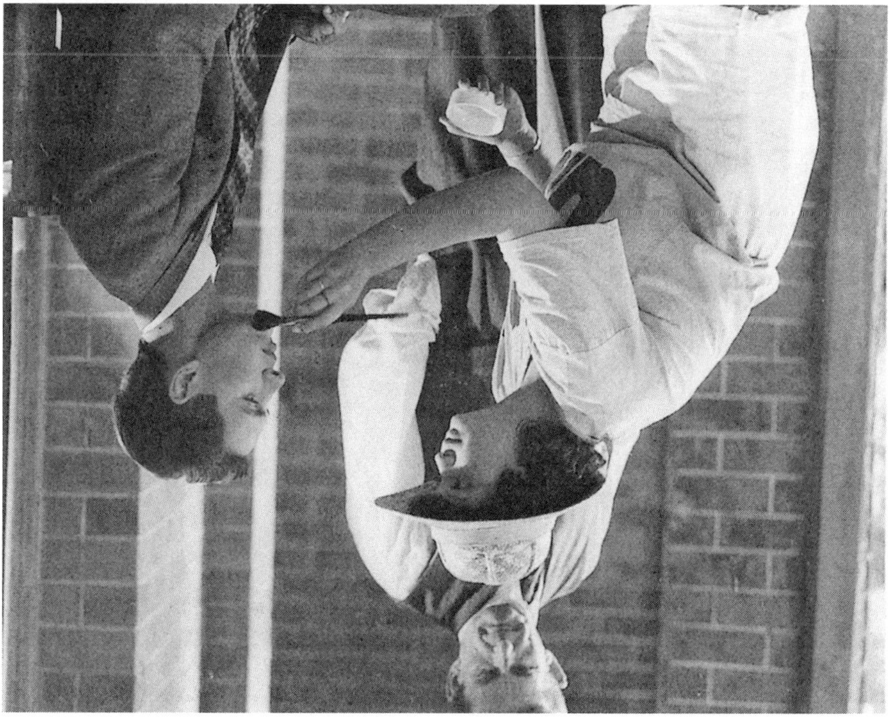

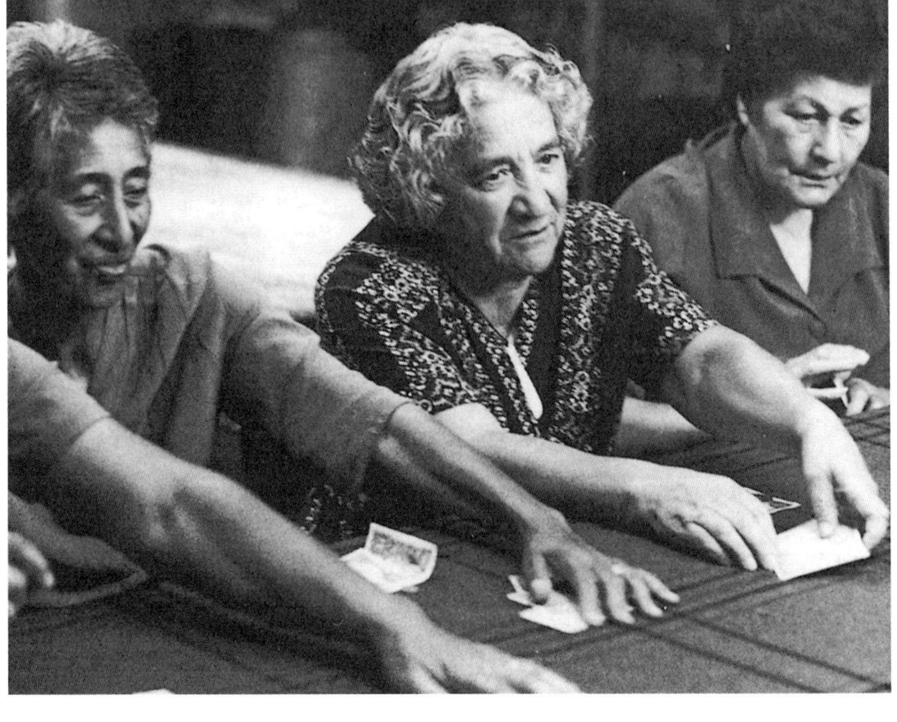

In the kitchen of Iritekura marae the women play cards in a scene of *Ngati*. Card schools are very popular in many rural Maori communities. They can be simply a chance to get together; they can also be an opportunity to raise funds for marae needs. From the left, Frances Harrison, Iranui Haig and Tangiwai Blane.

Pacific Films, John Miller

OPPOSITE: On location on *Ngati*. At top, make-up assistant Mary Whitlock brushes down lead actor Ross Girven who plays Greg, the young Australian sent back to the rural Maori community of Kapua by his father. Below, extras Michelle Walker (left) and Mereana Karauria watch the set-up.

Pacific Films, John Miller

OVER PAGE: In a scene from *Ngati* two youngsters (played by Peter McClutchie, on horseback, and Bruce Harrison) bring mutton carcasses along Waipiro Bay beach to the marae kitchen where they are carved up for the hangi (the traditional below-ground cooking pit) by (left to right) Lucky Renata, Kingi Karataina and Basil Grant.

Pacific Films, John Miller

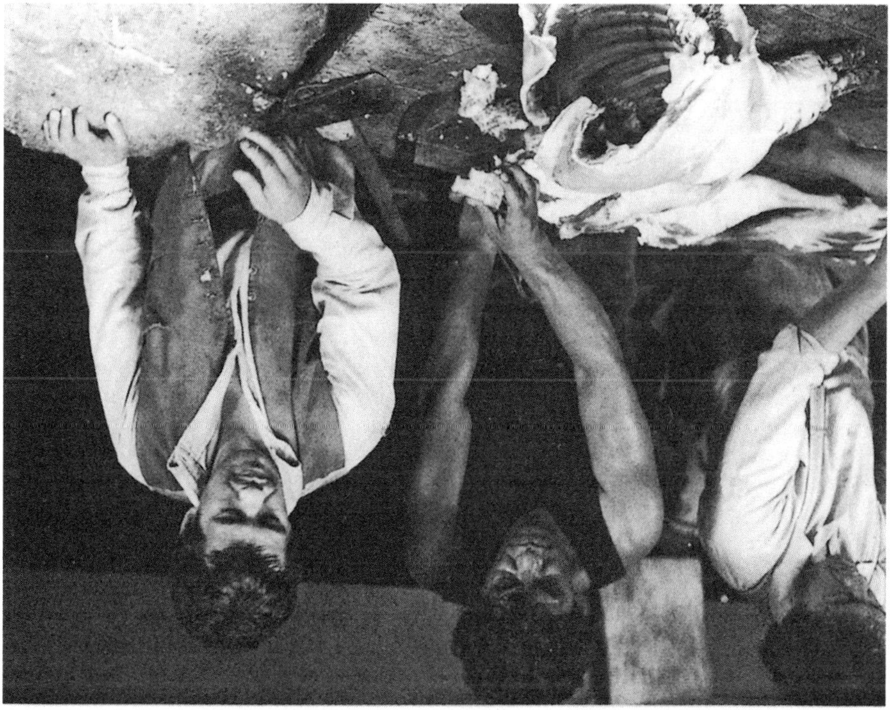

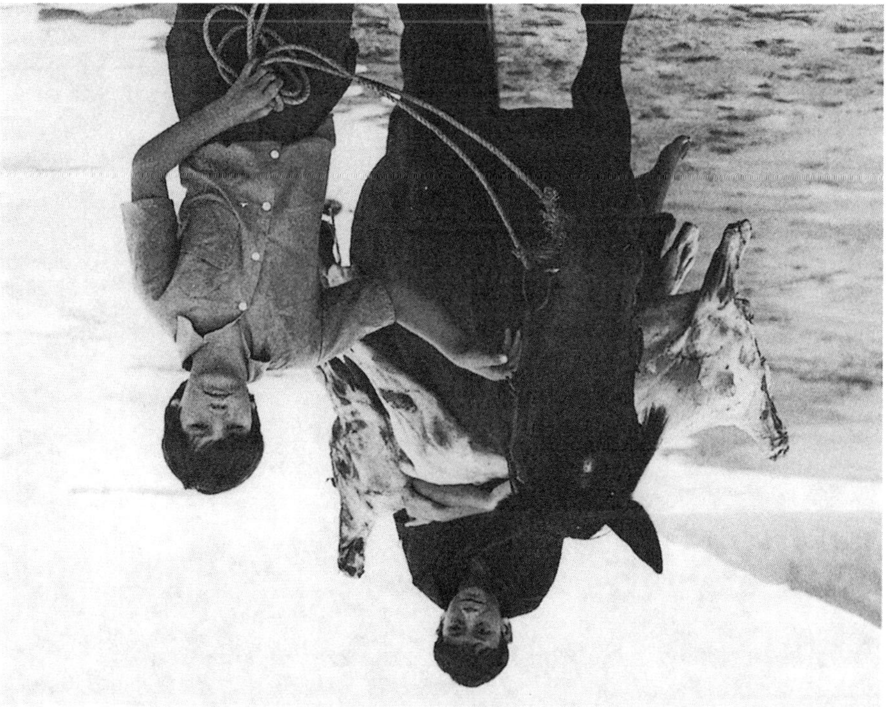

7

The Held Image

I wished I had never agreed to accompany *Ngati* to the Hawaiian island of Maui. I had just been through two weeks of having to talk on my feet after screenings on the islands of Oahu and Kauai, followed by interviews and hours of talk with native Hawaiian nationalists. The prospect of another week of the same made Maui seem one island too many. But there it was, stretching out from the airport, the mountains extravagant and the flats smacking of home. The roads were barely two-cars wide, cutting through fields of cane and with elbow-sharp turns constructed for reasons known only to some demented surveyor. The grazing lands of the Wairarapa where I grew up were similarly quirky.

The volunteers who staged the festival were like the country people I remember from my childhood days – down-to-earth and enormously solicitious. On the second day of my visit one of them asked me if I would mind talking to her pupils. "They don't know nothin' about anythin'," she said. She explained she was in charge of a school for kids thrown out from other colleges for being too rebellious. "They don't want to learn anythin' either." It was getting better and better. "And most of them are native Hawaiians." I agreed to show up at 10.30 next morning.

I was being put up in a ground floor unit built for the tourist trade. The condominiums were stacked mile upon mile along an impossibly beautiful beach and they were as tall as rockets about to lift off for Mars. The dozens of honeymooners on levels higher than mine appeared to be very literate. Around 7 a.m. one partner (almost never two together) would emerge onto the box balcony and read before, I supposed, a pre-breakfast dip.

My own apartment had its mysteries too. It was very much a couple's nest, there being only one broad bed. Yet there were two

back-to-back bathroom units – duplicate showers, mirrors and toilets. I paced out the length of the unit. One third of the floor space was taken up with the dual ablution block. It worried me, the thought of what kind of people might have slept side-by-side in my room and, come the morning, found it necessary to wash in places apart.

When we drove clear of the tourist belt, the volcano sat solid above the canefields. The school was hard to find. Dark men chatted on the red dust, nodding their heads "that way" to our request for directions. We passed a cane processing mill, a sprawling assemblage squirting steam that looked to me like a propped up junkyard. A wayside store, shamelessly unpainted. A cracked window behind which there might have been the smells of saddlery. The cane. And workers walking without much obvious purpose. The school, that place where they don't know nothin' about anythin', must be somewhere in there.

The first half hour of talk with the kids wasn't easy. I liked them – they were saucy young people who had had their troubles. However, it quickly became apparent that every question was going to be answered by their teacher. One boy asked what sort of fish we ate in New Zealand. The teacher said crayfish, a type of lobster. She had spent two weeks in New Zealand, and at Rotorua, one of our more important tourist spots, she had tasted crayfish and could explain what it looked like and how it tasted. I did everything I could to force the chat free of intervention. In fact I wound up drawing a map of our country on the board and showing where the best dope is said to grow. We checked out the likely penalties relative to our own countries and then the discussion shifted to whether our forest birds were colourful, and did we have reggae bands.

The young women received permission to leave early to collect the food for lunch. They rose as a group and were about to make for the door when one paused and addressed me directly. "Can I show you my girl?" I nodded. As her friends gathered in behind her, she reached under her desk and pulled out a large (about two feet square) photograph, in colour, framed and with a glass cover. The studio-lit toddler was in a pressed shirt, with hands clapping. The 14-year old mother, surrounded by her friends, looked so proud. I mumbled a few words. How old was her child? Was she allowed to bring her child to

class? (No, of course). I told her what a lucky woman I thought she was to have such a child. Other things, I suppose. But the truth of it was that I did not know which way to turn my eyes.

It seemed to me that, in one gesture, a "know nothin' about anythin'" child was showing something remarkable about how we collect and save our images, about how we present them and to whom. It also staggered me how what the youngster was doing among the canefields of Maui – beyond the condominiums, beneath the volcano – was so true to the way I have seen images held and presented at times in the Maori community, whether on the coastal flats of Ngati Porou, or under the protecting mists of Maungapohatu. On the face of it, that young mother standing there in her poor clothes had little to give anybody – and yet she was so upright among her "cousins", presenting flesh and blood to an outsider that no state authority, no academic, no communicator, or no archivist could take from her. It was her image. She was holding it.

The very mechanisms and the cost of film-making turns one into a robber of sorts. You can take a polaroid camera along to the first birthday party of a niece and leave the snaps taken with the parents. Years later the image, stained with age, might be taken from a grandmother's handbag or a father's wallet, to be shown to somebody sitting in the next seat in a bus. But with film, each day's snaps are taped in cans by the camera assistant and flown out to the nearest laboratory. The image has left the area and will probably never return.

Of course the normal decencies of pre-production should ensure that if robbery really is involved, then at least it is robbery with the consent of the people being "robbed". Unfortunately, that does not always happen. Too often images are obtained by smooth talk, banter or bullying. But in spite of this, most good film-makers go to great lengths to make it clear to the community in general, and to those who will eventually appear on screen in particular, the framework within which they will appear. The crew still spend time obtaining permission to take pictures.

"Taking Pictures!" – John O'Shea loathes that phrase. I recall him explaining why back in the early 70s, when we were both involved in making the *Tangata Whenua* series. He sticks firmly to the same line

to this day: "We do not take pictures. People give us pictures." Semantics? Some cute aphorism from an Eastern religion? Not for me. Not any longer anyway. I have been given too many pictures.

The last programme of the *Tangata Whenua* series deals with some core Maori principles – wairua, mauri, tapu – principles that are not talked about very frankly with outsiders in public. I was hoping that Ngati Porou leader Ngoi Pewhairangi might contribute to the programme.

We based the crew in the area for a week or so and filmed support sequences. I had talked on my own with Ngoi about what sort of material I thought was important for the theme of the programme, knowing full well how personal the request was, and knowing too that Ngoi would weigh what was being asked of her with great care. One morning towards the end of our stay, Ngoi said to me, "Come on. Now. We'll do it." We immediately set up the equipment in the meeting house and filmed Ngoi recounting, amongst other things, a very private memory of how "breaking tapu" can mean loss of life.

To the casual viewer her contribution might appear just another folksy tale, but not to Maori viewers. Ngoi knew exactly what she was doing. And I am sure the whole crew knew, and know to this day, that we were not taking pictures that morning – we were being given them. I have many recollections of that kind.

So we came to take the images back to the editing room in the city, a full day's hard driving away. What with deadlines and travel costs there is little real hope that we can simply pop back to show people what they have gifted. Overnight we become custodians of other people's spirits.

Although we would like to pretend otherwise, our time with the images will be fleeting – three months, six months, a year at the most. There will be an intensive period of editing while we polish the images to a fine sheen. We will try to get a near-finished edit back to the area, to check whether we might have done something crass, and then we will hand the finished product over for transmission. We will move on too, to be gifted images in other areas on other themes and, like it or

not, our memories will dim and so will the memories of those who gifted the images. The people will say to camera teams coming in three or four years later, "We had a film crew up this way. They took shots of the mountain, and of our school jubilee. Not sure how long ago that was. They filmed my grannie too, Are you from the same crowd?" The image will have slipped from their grasp.

As technicians with some pride in our craft, we will have done our best to keep the material in good shape, not letting it out to any comer. This is not quite as straightforward as it sounds – storage space will be limited and usually not very satisfactory for the long-term maintenance of what are, by their nature, perishable materials. And two or three times a year we may get a telephone call from some current affairs producer who wants, say, shots of a tangi (funeral).

"What sort of a tangi?"

"It doesn't matter really, just a tangi."

Our tactics are to say that we have to refer back to the elders in the tribal area, a process that might take a couple of weeks. The producer finds the shots of a tangi that were thought to be essential are no longer essential after all.

The conventional wisdom of the majority culture tells us that in order to rid ourselves of our worries about our inadequacy as custodians of other people's image-gift, we have only to pass the material over to a film archive. Trained people will preserve the material and make it available under whatever conditions we lay down. That should work, shouldn't it? A safe home-away-from-home, and a perpetual one at that. Or does such an archivist's vault merely serve to remove the image still further from the descendants of those who gave it?

Tuhoe hunters in the Urewera told me that if one of their dogs killed a wild pig, instead of pinning it down until the hunter arrived to "stick it", the hunter would chop a couple of inches off the dog's tail. Each time the dog offended, another couple of inches would come off. "That's why you see so many dogs with short tails around here." Or the dead pig would be lashed to the dog's back and the dog abandoned in the bush. Struggling under the weight, the dog usually made it

back home in four or five days, starving and chastened. Wild country – wild people.

Well, that's how it might look to a travel writer dropped in on an assignment by some glossy foreign magazine. For myself, the weeks I have spent working in Tuhoe have been amongst my happiest times in film-making. The people there have a healthy suspicion of outsiders – understandable, when they have spent so many years being robbed in one way or another, including being robbed by ethnographers, recordists, and picture-takers like myself. But once the people have had an opportunity to size you up, they are enormously hospitable. They are also steeped in their tribal traditions, having been forced to stand their ground in their mountains while the invader culture wreaked civilisation upon the more accessible lands of other tribes.

The Natural History Unit of Television New Zealand was planning a series of six 50-minute programmes on our national parks, one of which is the Urewera National Park, the homeland of the Tuhoe people. The producer of the series, Neil Harraway, approached me and asked would I direct the Urewera programme? I weighed that one up pretty carefully, worrying perhaps about losing a couple of inches off my tail.

I discussed a number of conditions with Neil: trained Maori technicians should be invited onto the crew, and a Maori style of pre-production should be used. I also asked whether we might explore a way of getting the most important images back into the hands of Tuhoe. Some extra cost would be involved but, on the other hand, we might be able to get material that would be of more substance than material given to a crew that simply dropped in from the sky, stayed a few days, left, and returned nothing. Neil agreed.

It is no fun standing in your socks on a mat in a meeting house in Tuhoe, using English to try to convince the old people that you really are going to bring the pictures back. They have heard plenty of that sort of enthusiastic talk over the decades. I think the old people thought, "Well, here is another liar, but maybe – just maybe – something will come of it this time."

When the Urewera footage came into the editing room, it was turned into the sort of scrambled eggs editors are familiar with. Before

editing can begin the sound is transferred off the $^1/4$ inch tape used on location on to 16mm magnetic stock, which is sprocketed exactly like film stock. A colour workprint is taken off the processed camera negative that has been exposed on location and, by a system of chopping out and adding in, the sprocketed sound is lined up with the workprint image, so that the picture and sound can run through the editing machines in synchronisation. It can be seen as a thankless task, syncing rushes, but once the job is done you have the satisfaction of seeing, for the first time, the image jump into life with sound.

The rushes are then broken down into shots. At every place where the camera was started or stopped both the image and sound are cut, precisely in sync, and the picture and sound are rolled together into one roll, held together with a rubber band, before taping an identification across the roll. After breaking down the rushes of a 50-minutes documentary you may wind up with 300-400 rolls, each labelled with "gobbledegook", like 132-2. Some rolls will be as big as a dinner plate, others button-sized. The rolls are packed neatly into large cans, 30 to a can, and labelled with further gobbledegook – such as "Wai talk SI.86-1 to 91-3."

Scrambled eggs – or at least that is what it looks like to casual visitors to the editing room, yet the editing team can put a finger on every image at a moment's notice. The editor might say to an assistant, "Can you get me the shot of the boot going into the stirrup?" Woe betide the assistant who can't find the image within 30 seconds. Just to complicate the ordered scrambled eggs further, the editing team generally cuts off what are called head and tail extensions and rolls them up separately.

Sound extensions occur because while the sound is usually run continuously during an interview on location, the camera may be switched on only intermittently. A conversation with an elder may continue for an hour or more, while the camera has run for only 15 minutes. Before the rushes make it to the editing room all of the sound – the whole hour-plus of it – will have been transferred onto 16mm sprocketed sound tape and presented to the editing team for syncing – heaps of sound with relatively little picture to go with it.

Faced with large amounts of sound without picture, there are two

ways for the editing team to go. The pictureless sound can be wound up into a separate roll and given a mystery number, such as H122-2. This sound is very important and the editing team will keep careful track of it. For example, an anecdote told in both picture and sound about, say, "the morning I found Granny's cow eating my poppies" might begin in picture-with-sound as "that cow just stood there. She seemed to be laughing at me."

To make sense of the story, introductory lines will have to be found somewhere in the sound-without-picture roll – in the sound head extension. One line might be found near the beginning of the roll – "The cow that Granny bought from Joe Harris kept breaking into my garden." At another place in the roll – "Last Friday morning I was going out to hose down the shed, and there she was, eating my poppies." These wild lines can be strung together under mute shots to kick the story off, so that in the finished edit it would flow thus: "The cow that Granny bought from Joe Harris kept breaking into my garden. Last Friday morning I was going out to hose down my shed, and there she was, eating my poppies. That cow just stood there. She seemed to be laughing at me."

The other way for the editing team to go is to leave the sound head-and-tail extensions attached to the picture-with-sound roll. One picture-with-sound shot might be only 30 seconds long, but with head-and-tail sound extensions it might wind up being five minutes long. And to make it possible for the 30-second picture-with-sound section to go through the editing machines in sync, junk film will have to be added to the picture roll to build it out from 30 seconds to five minutes. The junk film is called "filler" or "gash", and is not cheap. Usually it will be waste film from another production. Some pretty weird things can happen when you put gash with wild sound. Viewing rushes, I have heard an old man talking about Maori determination to have control over marae-based housing, while seeing on the screen an inverted image of a young woman fastening her bra – waste footage from a talent test for a commercial.

This then is the fate of images and sound recorded in the field: carefully tagged rolls in some dozens of cans, every frame logged, cared for, but removed from the tribe. If one day you should visit

Wellington, you could check it out for yourself. You could walk into our editing room and try to locate a shot of a boot going into a stirrup, or an elder talking about marae-based housing. A trained assistant editor supplied with the paperwork could do it, but not the rest of humanity – not even those who recorded the material in the field.

On the Urewera film the editing team reassembled a portion of the umpteen rolls that resulted from the breaking-down of the rushes. This was done before the edit began and was a first step towards returning something to Tuhoe. We were very selective: only images and sound of the elders speaking in Maori were reassembled. The kids kicking a football, a 12-year old carrying a deer he had shot out of the bush, a wood pigeon eating, a pensioner raking lawn clippings – these images were left in their small rolls. The footage of the elders talking in Maori was assembled into separate rolls, one roll per elder. All sound relevant to each roll – with head-and-sound extensions – was included in the reassembled rolls. Costly white spacer, rather than junk images from another production, was used as gash. Then a video copy was made of each roll, and television's Natural History Unit funded me to take the tapes back to the elders who had been interviewed. I gave the video tapes, not to the tribal authority, not to the local marae committee, not to the local school, but to each elder personally.

Once the reassembled rolls had been copied onto video they were broken down again and editing began. In my innocence, I had imagined that the barefoot doctor "archiving" process I have just recounted would be simple to carry through – low-cost, and neither time-consuming nor disruptive to the edit. But I did not appreciate just how contrary to current craft practices my scheme was. I came to feel like a young man who unwittingly does something indelicate in the centre of the ballroom.

For starters, I had it explained to me that it is not proper – from an archivist's point of view – to favour some material ahead of other material. To do that is to be taking an editorial stance in the present, a stance that others at some future date might find unsatisfactory. If we were going to take a back-up copy of some of the images we had gathered in the field, images of leaders speaking Maori in this case, then we should make copies of all the material. I get a little short-

tempered with that argument. I get even more short-tempered when it is implied that perhaps my focus as director leaves me poorly equipped to gauge the relative value of material for future generations – as if you weren't making that sort of judgment every hour you spend directing a crew on location.

Well, sorry. Thanks to years of image control exercised by the majority culture there are precious few Maori images at all. It is just a bit much for the majority culture to pontificate now on which Maori images the Maori community should give priority to saving.

Certainly, I can see that a casually-shot image of a young girl riding her horse down a street in the Tuhoe village of Waimana (a shot which was taken to provide what film-makers rather coldly call "wallpaper") could possibly be of great value to some researcher doing a thesis in 2010 on the changing face of New Zealand rural towns. The appearance of the houses. Were there hedges and fruit trees? And so-called wallpaper images will some day be treasured by the local people too, especially by the immediate family. "I didn't know you used to ride to school, granny."

But what is all of that compared with images of the last of the Tuhoe elders who collected the now protected kereru (wood pigeon) under the old rules, speaking in the Tuhoe dialect about the traditional rituals, strictures and hunting and cooking methods associated with kereru? The Tuhoe people are arguably the last of our country's forest dwellers, with a knowledge of their immediate environment that a couple of centuries back must have been every bit as intimate as that of the famous desert-dwelling bushmen of the Kalahari. Furthermore, the Maori language is spoken nowhere else but in New Zealand and the Cook Islands, yet I doubt whether there is more than a few minutes of film depicting senior Maori speakers talking in their own language that we, as technicians, can guarantee to be printable in five, let alone fifty years' time. To my way of thinking, there is a tragedy occurring right under our noses, and the girl on the horse can wait a little for attention. I am sure if the case were put to the people in Waimana they would agree.

To transfer our selection of Urewera material to video took a full day in a transfer suite, a costly exercise. To transfer all the material

(picture and sound) would have taken a week, an impossible burden on any documentary production. In the end, if you try to save everything, you might wind up saving nothing.

Another point of discussion in putting the video records together after the Urewera shoot concerned head-and-tail sound extensions. The editing team questioned whether it was really necessary to include these extensions, turning what might be no more than a 30-second picture-with-sound clip into a five-minute roll. A conversation with one elder might – with head-and-tail sound extensions included – run to two hours, whereas a picture/sound-only roll might be less than half an hour. Obviously there are cost implications – the amount of gash and video tape needed, and studio transfer time.

I mentioned earlier that people working in the editing room take great care of head-and-sound extensions. On the other hand, the extensions (and on some documentaries there can be hours of them) are a bit like a bits-and-pieces shed at the back of a panelbeater's workshop – a place to be visited only when you can't find just the right nut. The fewer times the editing team has to trip into the shed the better, but you maintain the shed with its bits and pieces in good shape against the day you are caught short for a suitable introductory or bridging line, a suitable atmosphere or a sound effect.

However, in the particular case of the Urewera project, the bits-and-pieces shed contains talk of great importance to Tuhoe, material every bit as valuable as that which came to be showcased (with picture) in the completed programme, or in the picture-with-sound clips rolled up in the editing cans. Fair enough, the editing team said, but the bits-and-pieces sound is not going to be tossed out. It will always exist in the master sound tapes and should anybody in the future want to look into all the material in any depth, they would only have to play over the master tapes. And there's the rub. To get into the $1/4$ inch masters and to locate material of interest in them, you have to have access to replay equipment and you have to be able to fight your way through paper records which, though crystal clear to a specialist, are like low night fog on a country road for most of us.

The sound of your elders talking is locked away in small cardboard boxes in a city vault awaiting some magical future time when – in the

style of boys' adventure stories of old – a man gritted by sand levers up the stone to reveal a snake-infested space housing crafted metals never touched by white hands. And in the background the native bearers cheer.

Our editing crew also questioned whether it was necessary to make up a separate roll for each elder. Preparing separate rolls takes a little more time in the editing room because leaders and tails have to be on a number of rolls instead of on one large roll, and each roll has to be individually marked up and given its own can. Separate rolls make for a great deal more time and expense when it comes to transferring on to video, because each image/sound roll has to be separately laced on the transfer machine and a fresh cassette inserted. How much simpler and cheaper to make up a single image/sound roll and transfer everything on to one large video cassette for return to the Tuhoe people.

The trouble is that the perception of the Tuhoe people as some collective mass audience is a myth. Each elder we interviewed has his or her genealogical bonds to this or that family, and to this or that part of the mountains and rivers of the Tuhoe homeland. There are organisations which operate as a collective front for the whole of Tuhoe, or for major portions of it – the Tuhoe Trust Board, the various marae committees, and even the local schools, the football clubs, the work training centres, and the hunting association. But these are functional bodies which have evolved because of the need for the traditional whanau (extended family) system to have some sort of voice in the majority culture's corridors of power. To return the image to such functional bodies (as we would have had to do if the material of the elders was butted end-to-end in a roll) would seem to me to be playing along with exactly that sort of alienation process that appears to be fundamental to the way the majority culture gathers and circulates images. The image is public and its destiny is mass circulation to a common audience.

The mists were elsewhere when cameraman Swami Hansa and I drove back into Tuhoe to get our landscape scenes – mute shots of the lake,

the kereru cracking the miro berries, the mountain streams twisting over rocks. On the Waimana river flats cows were being driven in for milking and kids were flying their kites in the school playground. The camera equipment was tightly packed in the back of the van. Between Hansa and me sat six video tape cassettes, one tape for each elder interviewed two months earlier.

We found Mau Rua crutching ewes in his shearing shed. We found Nino easily too. He usually lives across the river, in a small shack under a bush ridge accessible only by wading, but on this clear morning he was up by the road staying with his young relations. He is an imposing man, Nino, with such a flow of white hair and such a darkness of features that a casting director looking for a man to play a guru running an ashram in Goa would sign him up on the spot. Swami Hansa and I leaned on the rusted fence and I handed the tape across to Nino – the tape of what he had given to our film (picture and all the sound).

Over the next few days we delivered tapes to all the elders who had taken part in the filming. Handing those tapes across one by one to each elder became some of the most special moments I have ever had in film-making. Part of it was knowing I was keeping the trust ("that fella didn't turn out to be a liar after all") and part of it was seeing the pride in those old people's eyes. Like the young woman in the canefields of Maui, they were holding their own image in their own hands. I told them that only one copy had been made of the material. Nobody – not the marae committee, not the university, not the Queen of England – could get a copy without their permission.

Two months later I was back in Tuhoe and dropped in on some of those elders. There were the tapes, with pride of place on the shelf, and I heard the words that I was later to hear on Maui, in an only slightly different form – "You wanna see our koro?"

Does any of this have the slightest relevance to the proper long-term storage of picture/sound images of our people? Simply taking one fragile $^1/2$ inch video copy off workprint and delivering it to an old man in a woolshed in the bush does not seem to be a very serious way to go about archiving. But the problem at present is that people do not get an opportunity to see and hear what they donated, except for that

small portion which winds up in the finished edit, a much abridged version and one that has been ordered to suit the immediate needs of one team of programme makers. With the Urewera material the families had their images – all the most important ones – in their own homes, for at least a short time.

At any point the video tapes might be sent to relations in Sydney, or get so much playing among friends in the same valley that it will become damaged beyond repair. Yet the family will have glimpsed the image. In due course some youngster who has become active in marae affairs, or who has had university training might say to him or herself, "I've seen film of my grandfather talking about that," and have the drive to search out the original material preserved by the professionals in city-based institutions.

It is a thrill to know that at least some of the images of Tuhoe have been lifted out of the cans of scrambled eggs. It was made possible through having had a very sympathetic unit in television – one that has earned itself a touch of autonomy because of the quality of its work over the years – and having been blessed with an editing team, led by senior editor Simon Reece, that was patient enough to figure out the details of what were, for us, new rules, some of which ran right across ordinary editing room practices. I think something similar should be put in place on any documentary involving conversations of substance with the elders talking in the language. Some system of archiving-in-the-present is technically possible, and funding can be found to support it. The only obstacles are notional.

Film archiving, both technical and cultural, now has a tradition on an international basis. While we have much to gain from its dedication and expertise, the tradition seems to run contrary to some Maori ways of thinking. The New Zealand Film Archive has been exemplary as far as Maori material recorded some decades back goes. The director, Jonathan Dennis, along with a kuia (elder), Witarina Harris, who acts as guide for the archive on Maori material, have striven to take the stored material out to the Maori community, where it has been much appreciated. When I talk of Maori material in this context, I am talking about film taken by Pakeha people 50 or 60 years ago. While some of that material is pictorially exquisite, it does tend to be ethnographic,

with natives in native dress blowing a flute and so on. Nevertheless, much of the imagery is priceless and I believe the Maori community trusts the Archive to preserve and present that material in an appropriate way. I have been present at one or two Film Archive screenings of Maori material and can assure you they are magical.

We are actively encouraged to hand over our own Maori images to the Film Archive, but some of us are hesitant. One reason is that, like any archive in the world, an archive can seem to be like a tomb. (Museum curators, archivists and other professionals call it a vault.) You pass the material over to the tomb and some time in the distant future somebody, and it is very likely to be a Pakeha, will reassemble the material and parade it in a way that may, or may not, meet the needs of the Maori community at that time.

In the past, Maori stored food under very strict rules. It would be unconscionable for a food-gatherer to toss food into the storage pit without making sure that it was properly prepared for the future. That is exactly what we are being urged to do by the Archive, which is happy enough to take in all film or film-related material. This material often arrives in fractured form – sound trims, picture trims, paper records from the editing room hastily stapled together, and the negatives. It need not be that way. There is no time that a film is better known than at the conclusion of an edit and we have argued that this is the time to prepare the food for storage.

When I was in Honolulu with *Ngati* I attended a meeting of film archive administrators from various countries, primarily to discuss a proposal to set up a film and video archive in Hawaii. This archive could have great relevance to the peoples of the Pacific, and the international team was floating ideas to stimulate the two people charged with setting up the Hawaiian archive. When I said that at home we would like to look hard at archiving-in-the-present, I was told that they would all like to make oral history recordings. One participant talked about an idea he had had to record some of the old men in Hawaii talking about what it was like to work in the island's canefields as a young white man.

Now that phrase "oral history" gets to me. I have done oral history recording, as it is understood by the majority culture, when I worked

on a radio station in my early twenties. I was on the station when Russian Jack, one of our last itinerant hobos, or swaggies as we call them, was recorded. Invariably, when we express a wish to save material of the elders talking in the language, we are put on the same footing as recordists wishing to save the chat from Russian Jack. It can be even worse than that, for people get this vision of Maori wanting to trek around the land filming every Maori grannie in sight. If they allow that, are they not going to have to also allow elders from our small Italian community in Wellington to speak for hours about how to make cane lobster pots in the traditional way?

Despite having been involved on a good number of occasions in discussions with archivists from the majority culture, I do not have a ready answer as to why oral history recordings should be different for Maori and Pakeha. They are different. We have simple words for it among ourselves. "This is a recording of your kaumatua." This means a great deal more than announcing to a Pakeha that you have some historic recordings of Russian Jack, but for the life of me I cannot see a way to explain the difference to the majority culture.

Perhaps that is what is at the heart of many of our problems in attempting to develop communication forms within the majority culture. Even when there is the greatest of goodwill on both sides, our country's two cultures simply do not speak the same language. And this example of a common mental landscape is just the tip of the iceberg.

What if one really uses Maori thinking on saving things of value for the future? Maori tradition tells us there is a time for some things to be left in peace to die. You can see evidence of this on many family lands. Often enough, a disused house is left in the field to quietly fall down. It is not bulldozed into oblivion, nor is the roofing iron carted away to cover a new pig pen. There are a host of deep-seated spiritual reasons for leaving a house that way, and no amount of sneering from Pakeha neighbours about "typical untidy Maoris" will persuade a family to dismember an old family building. It even applies to cars. When you come to our country you will see rusted family cars sitting in their last glory among the weeds – they have not been disembowelled for spare parts.

Conversely, some items are fiercely protected. In fact, to abuse a treasure by removing it from where it has been placed for storage would almost certainly lead to some calamity befalling you or your immediate family. At least, that is what many Maori believe. These are not obscure matters to Maori people. You do not have to go to university to learn about them, you do not have to seek the advice of anthropologists. They are part of daily Maori life and are referred to in everyday speech. But when you come to talk through a more appropriate Maori film archiving system with Pakeha friends who have never encountered such common Maori thoughts, you feel you are talking to people from Jupiter.

When I was in Hawaii, the New Zealand Film Archive was also there screening the McDonald films, a series of short government-funded documentary clips shot between 1919 and 1923 by the Pakeha film-maker, James McDonald. Despite the camera being a bit like an outsider peering into Maori rural life as it was then, the images have great beauty; they are priceless for ethnographers and very moving for the Maori community, who can feel the presence of their immediate ancestors in much the way they sense their presence in carvings in the meeting house – which to many outsiders are nothing more than sculptures. I went to two of the screenings of the McDonald films in Hawaii, and what a special treat that was.

The director of the New Zealand Film Archive helped introduce the films and then handed proceedings over to the Maori kuia, Witarina Harris. Witarina makes an indelible impression wherever she goes to support the showing of Maori images, and despite some infirmity she has always been on call to give that touch to a Maori event that can come only from the qualities that elders bring with them. A recent hip operation meant she had to use a wheelchair, but when important points had to be made she rose to her feet and, with a mixture of shrewd humour and immense dignity, she would answer in a way that won the hearts of all. She made me proud to be there.

The McDonald films continued to be screened in Hawaii and eventually I wound up on the canefields on Maui, and on that same day that the young woman was showing me her studio photograph of her child, archival images of Maori people were being screened on the

big island of Hawaii. I can't help feeling there is a mighty contradiction in there somewhere.

Come one hundred years, I hope there will be some way the images that have been given to me can be held up by the people themselves, on their own lands. For that to happen we are going to have to continue the slow process of marrying together the archival skills of the majority culture with Maori knowledge of what spirit shines from the held image.

Barry Barclay (Ngāti Apa, 1944–2008) was one of the most influential filmmakers in New Zealand. His films include the award-winning *Ngati* (1987), *Te Rua* (1991), and *The Feathers of Peace* (2000). He was director of *Tangata Whenua,* the first television documentary series to present the Māori people to a mainstream audience. In 2007 he was made a Member of the Order of New Zealand (M.N.Z.M.) for his services to film.

Jeff Bear (Maliseet) is a writer and moving-image storyteller specializing in television documentary. He has worked on prime-time current affairs programs for the Canadian national networks CTV and CBC. As an independent producer, he focuses on indigenous stories and has produced for world indigenous networks APTN, NITV, and Māori Television.

AF478880